DELIGHTFUL DOLLS

ANTIQUE AND OTHERWISE

FANCHON

DELIGHTFUL DOLLS

ANTIQUE AND OTHERWISE

By

THELMA BATEMAN

PHOTOGRAPHS BY THE AUTHOR

1966

HOBBY HOUSE PRESS

461 BEN FRANKLIN STATION, WASHINGTON, D.C. 20044

Dedicated
To Doll Lovers
Everywhere

And to My Son

PREFACE

Dear Reader:

This book was approached from the standpoint that dolls are alive, little people—having feelings, personalities and idiosyncrasies of their own; that they *do* things or *refuse* to do them—just like children. James Schoenhut, for instance, kept me awake for hours one night jumping up and down on his bed until I finally silenced him by catching him in his act, with the camera!

My two little granddaughters, Janet and Gail Corwin, inadvertently reopened the doll world for me. The loss of a mother in their infancy released a flood of lovely gifts for them over the years. In coping with their many dolls and toys, I first fell in love with some of the exquisite modern dolls. Then, I began to remember the dolls and toys played with by my own daughter and son. The next step was remembering those of *my* childhood, and you can imagine what happened after that!

When the resulting doll collection needed cataloging, I bought a Polaroid 800—my first and only venture with a camera. I am indebted to my son, for it was he who taught me how to use the camera and then turned me loose to learn by doing.

The photographs and vignettes appearing in this book are limited to those of dolls which are still collectible today—with persistent hunting—and if one has helpful friends and a share of good luck. Many of the dolls and accessories pictured are from my collection. Most of the modern accessories are not mentioned since they are still easily available. For dolls appearing here who belong to others, credit is given at the end of each vignette. I am especially grateful to those who loaned their dolls. It's no small thing to part with a beloved child, even for a few days! The cooperation of those who helped me personally with gifts and loans of research material and allowed me to purchase out-of-print items, has been invaluable.

As you read the many references, you will realize how indebted we all are to people everywhere who have researched for years before, and to those who continue to dig! No doll book could be written without all kinds of help from other people. Consider the many from whom we learn just by being allowed to see their entire collections or to examine individual dolls. Then think of the many who generously tell of their findings at doll club meetings, informal get-togethers and even chance meetings! The truth is, it's possible to learn something from *every* contact. That's why there are no individual names here—the list would be impossibly long.

If you like our book (and it *is* "our" book) how about doing more? It's been fun.

Hoping to have been helpful and to have provided a piece or two to fit the fascinating "jig saw puzzle" of doll research, I remain . . .

Gratefully, affectionately and sincerely yours,

THELMA BATEMAN

Arleta, California
March, 1966

VIGNETTES AND ILLUSTRATIONS

VIGNETTES AND ILLUSTRATIONS

VIGNETTES AND ILLUSTRATIONS

VIGNETTES AND ILLUSTRATIONS

VIGNETTES AND ILLUSTRATIONS

VIGNETTES AND ILLUSTRATIONS

DELIGHTFUL DOLLS

ANTIQUE AND OTHERWISE

HUMILITY AND PATIENCE

Humility and Patience

J. D. Kestner Twins—24 Inch

THESE are the ones who started it all—if you know what I mean! In the back room of an antique shop I saw them, seated side by side in a child's old chair sleigh. They utterly fascinated me. I couldn't forget them. For months I kept saying to myself, "What in the world do you want with two old dolls?" However, using every excuse to re-visit the shop, I finally succumbed—dolls, chair sleigh and all.

The fact that they were identical in every respect, except mouths, and in such beautiful condition interested me most, I believe. Humility (left) has the closed mouth and Patience the open mouth, showing four nice even white teeth. Now they have new golden human hair wigs. Wish I had kept the blond mohair wigs which were sparse, but original. Ho-hum, we live and learn!

The twins' velvet coats and bonnets (with velvet flowers) are a lovely soft shade of medium green and their dresses are gold net with gold underslips—not original, but old. Both have white cotton socks and shoes with narrow pale green ribbon ties matching the yards of wide ribbon on their sashes and bonnets, quaint "Kate Greenaway" costumes.

Excelsior D.R.P. no. 70685 Germany is stamped in red ink on the small of their backs and the fully ball-jointed composition bodies are of fine quality. The heads are bisque—also fine quality—well modeled and softly tinted, complete with chin dimples. Their eyes are brown, sleeping and very large. Incised in back, under the wigs is:

K.   Made in   14
Germany

—an early Kestner marking, probably before 1896.

See: "Kestner Dolls" by Bullard and Callicot in *Spinning Wheel*, December, 1959.

Helen

Simon & Halbig—26½ Inch

Helen may not look it, but she is older than most all who read this book. *S. H. 1079—Dep. 13* is incised in script in the pale bisque of her head—'way up under the wig in back. Her body, of French-type construction, fully articulated, is unmarked. The upper and lower arms are wooden shafts with wooden balls at the elbow. Her upper legs are wood, with the ball on the upper end fastened to the shaft. Her composition torso has large open hip sockets and, while the thighs are rightfully hers, they fit loosely. Her hands, lower legs and feet are composition.

Helen's silver blond human hair is original, thick and lovely. It was washed (outdoors) through three pans of benzine. That way, the curl stays in. Not very dignified, having your hair hanging on the clothesline, but worth it in the long run!

She has pearl ear drops and necklace. Her brown sleeping eyes with real lashes, ridged eyebrows, pretty white teeth and big dimple, all accent her delicate face. Helen wears a white organdy frock with large bertha, lace trimmed. Her wide satin sash is rose-pink. They are old but not original.

Helen is an oldie, indicated by the script incising, body type, and lack of the word *Germany*.

She is now in the collection of Mrs. George D. Schelling of San Fernando, Calif.

See: "Simon and Halbig, Master Craftsmen" by Genevieve Angione in *Spinning Wheel*, Jan.–Feb., 1963.

Dream Baby

Armand Marseille—6½ Inch

The baby in Helen's lap is an Armand Marseille Dream Baby, tiny size. Her composition head is marked *A.M. Germany* in back, above the neck flange. She has composition hands with wee fingers outspread. Her cloth body (cotton stuffed) is quite grotesque—somewhat like cloth bodies on the Bye-Lo babies. We had to build up her toes with cotton to hold on the miniature white

DREAM BABY AND HELEN

hand crocheted booties! Dream Baby, in the mid-1920's, was one of Germany's answers to the popularity of Grace Putnam's Bye-Lo.

Her head is well modeled for a small composition dolly, with nice tinting of face and hair. Her brown glass eyes are stationary now.

Her soft pale blue dress and slip, lace trimmed, are new. Dream Baby's cap was once a crocheted nut cup!

See: Elizabeth A. Coleman. *Dolls—Makers and Marks*, pp. 4, 76, 77.

Margaret

M O A German Bisque—26 Inch

Margaret has a very rosy complexion, lovely brown sleep eyes, real lashes, four teeth and a nice smile.

M O A (in an eight-pointed star) *Germany—200—10* is incised on back of her head. She was made by Welsch and Company and many "M O A's" are also marked *Welsch.* Her fully jointed composition body is unmarked but nice. Welsch also made bisque shoulderheads with jointed kid bodies.

Margaret's beautiful auburn human hair wig looks lovely with the pink ruffled organdy dress and bright blue hand crocheted jacket. Shoes and socks are white.

A friend who sold dolls in a large store in Los Angeles for years said the "M O A's" were late dolls, made after World War I. This could be true as Margaret's high coloring may indicate a late doll, as bisques go.

Peter sits on Margaret's lap. Angela and Mimi are described elsewhere.

This pretty child plays piano nicely and practices without being coaxed. Other little girls take notice!

Margaret is now in the collection of Mrs. Stephen Salatich of Reseda, California.

Peter

J. D. Kestner All Bisque Baby—5½ Inch (seated)

Peter has no clothes. He sits "naked as a jay bird" under a glass bell. He *does* wear the Kestner crown label on his chest. Incising on back of the head *J. D. K.* and *Germany* would date him sometime after 1896.

Peter is jointed at neck, shoulders and hips. The bisque is pale and smooth, the modeling unusually nice and well proportioned, arms and legs baby-curved. Fingers and toes are quite realistic, with big toes upturned.

Peter's eyes are gray and sleep. His mouth is open-closed, with narrow gum lines, but no teeth. The wavy contoured baby cap looks like caracul, soft golden in color. Altogether, Peter's quite a guy!

ANGELA, MIMI, PETER AND MARGARET

MIMI AND ANGELA

Mimi
Simon and Halbig Walker—8 Inch

Mimi, tired from walking, sat down beside the bunny. Angela quietly waited for Mimi to catch her breath. That's when the camera caught them.

Mimi turns her head from side to side while carefully shifting her weight from one foot to the other. It happens because a heavy wire, connected to the legs, runs up through the neck and fastens to a cross-bar inside the head. She has a round paper label on her back which says *BREVETÉ—S.G.D.G.* She was assembled in France. Incised under her wig: *SIMON & HALBIG, S & H, Germany 3/0.*

Her dainty bisque head is nicely modeled and tinted with slightly open lips exposing tiny teeth. Her blue eyes sleep and her light brown mohair is original.

Mimi has a slender, well-shaped papier-mâché body, jointed at shoulders and hips. Black socks are painted. Two strap slippers with low heels are molded and are painted luggage tan.

She is a clean child and her white nainsook dress and underclothes, lace trimmed, are spotless. However, I'm not sure about this sitting-on-the-grass business!

Angela
Bébé Steiner—8½ Inch

Steiner—*Paris*—A.1. is incised on back of Angela's pretty bisque head. Her blond mohair wig (cork cap) is original, mouth closed, blown glass blue eyes are stationary. Ears are pierced and applied. Painted eyelashes are typically Steiner, made with heavier, longer strokes, each stroke wider apart than on most French dolls.

Her compact composition body is jointed at hips and shoulders. On one side of her tummy is stamped in blue ink:
LE PETIT PARISIEN
BÉBÉ STEINER
Médaille d'Or
Paris 1889

Angela's tam and crocheted dress are white, with cerise ribbons. Wee ribbed socks and white kid slippers are original—sole stamped *BAU-DICH.*

"*Sea Song*"   GISÈLE

Gisèle
French Bisque—24 Inch

GISÈLE may be a maverick (that is, unmarked) and her panties just won't stay up, but she is so photogenic it's hard to keep the camera off her. Always ready for anything, that's my Gisèle! You should hear her play fiddle—on second thought, better not.

Her dark brown eyes are enormous, blown glass and stationary. Well—that's what it says here, but she never misses a trick. How she sees all and knows all without moving her eyes, I'll never know! Her short black human hair wig (cork cap) suits her perfectly, although new from Paris. The bisque head is smooth, mouth closed, chin dimpled. There is the artist's red mark on the back of her head M (or) N (or) H and VI.

Her clothes are original, except for the pinafore. The buff-toned cotton print of her dress is calico-like with tiny fine red lines. It is long-sleeved and low waisted, with full pleated skirt on which is wide lace, laid on flat. The dainty white pinafore dresses her up a bit, it's so lacy and all handmade.

Bright blue earrings match color with her quaint necklace. Hanging from a blue beaded chain are ten ceramic-petalled forget-me-nots, the gift of a friend. Her old black slippers are scuffed—wouldn't you know it?—and her lace socks white—when bleached, that is!

Gisèle's stocky French papier-mâché body is fully articulated (good thing for her) with large hands and thick fingers. She has been around a long time, *n'est-ce pas?*

"Encore?"   MARGARET AND GISÈLE

"Sunday School"   HELEN, THELMA-MARIE, HUMILITY AND PATIENCE

Lisette

French Bisque—Jumeau—20 Inch

THIS little girl looks like an angel with wings, but she isn't. Guess who let the parrot escape!

Lisette's beautiful head (incised X. 9) with artist's red mark L, is of smooth pale bisque with the darkest blue eyes—hand blown and stationary. The eyebrows are daintier, more delicately colored than usual. Her applied ears are works of art in themselves. The mouth is closed, nostrils and inner eye corners are pink tinted. Her earrings are tiny gold hearts.

Is she all Jumeau? I think so. Her early type papier-mâché body (no wrist joint) is stamped *JUMEAU-Médaille d'Or-Paris.* This probably refers to the earliest Paris gold medal award in 1878.

Lisette's red-brown human hair curls (cork pate) are a good foil for her delicate appearance—what with her old white dress, gray-blue velvet sash and ribbons. The pink hat was contrived from an old jabot.

Someone in the early 1900's spent many loving hours on her little dress, for which I am grateful. There are yards and yards of beautiful lace, insertion and embroidery. Only the waist in back and the underpart of the sleeves is soft handkerchief lawn. Her hand crocheted socks were originally my gloves from China—her little new white shoes are kid.

The gray chair, part of a set, was made at the turn of the century, probably by Mason and Parker.

See: Nina S. Davies. *The Jumeau Doll Story,* p. 79.
    Luella T. Hart. *Complete French Doll Directory,* pp. 31, 47.
    Inez and Marshall McClintock. *Toys in America,* p. 169.

LISETTE

LISETTE, GISÈLE, GENEVIÈVE, THELMA-MARIE (seated)

LISETTE

"Once Upon a Time"   LISETTE WITH DOLORES, MIMI, JIP, ANGELA AND HENRIETTA

GERDA

Gerda
Armand Marseille—8½ Inch

Gerda is all original and then some —meaning, of course, her trunk of extra clothes. The ones she wears are commercially made, the rest are homemade, but long ago. The heavy brown silk coat and matching tam, for instance, are stiff with age. She has two extra dresses; one pale pink cotton, and one party dress of white chiffon trimmed with narrow figured pink ribbon. There is an ivory wool coat, tiny white bib-apron, paper fan, straw hat, muff and fur, wee lace hankie, blue striped flannel nightie, blue crocheted slippers, extra underclothes and a velvet and lace drawstring bag to match the dress and velvet hat she wears.

Gerda's dress is ivory satin, full pleated from the belt down with a large salmon-pink velvet collar, lace trimmed. Her stockings are white cotton; slippers are white kid with large buckles.

She does her long light brown mohair in a typically German fashion, parted, braided and curled in a bun over each ear.

Gerda's smooth bisque head is highly colored but carefully done. Good modeling, open mouth, four tiny teeth and sleeping gray eyes. Under her wig is incised *Made in Germany*. On back of her head is 390—A. 11/0 M. Body is composition, fair quality, jointed at hips and shoulder.

There is a picture in *Ladies Home Journal* for May, 1915, showing a spring table decoration. In the center is a doll like Gerda; same size, same hairdo and a dress with a large square collar—lace trimmed—very similar to Gerda's. I believe both dolls date a bit earlier because of World War I. Anyway, it was fun to find this illustration and every bit helps when researching.

Thelma-Marie

Bébé Jumeau—24 Inch

Tʜɪꜱ Bébé Jumeau has two large doll trunks crammed with lovely old French clothes, most of them hand-made, plus dozens of accessories. Check the complete list at the end of this vignette.

Thelma-Marie has a beautiful bisque head, secured to her fully-jointed papier-mâché body by a hook fastened into a block of wood in her chest. Her enormous full blown glass eyes are dark brown and stationary. Her original human hair wig (cork cap) is golden-blond, still beautiful and luxuriant. The modeling of her features is lovely, ears pierced and applied, dots in nostrils and inner eye corners, mouth closed. There's a deep dimple in her chin and one under her nose. Stamped in red on the back of the neck is *Déposé Tête Jumeau Bté S.G.D.G.-11-*. Although jointed at the wrists, hands and fingers are quite large and thick. Stamped in blue ink on her back is *JUMEAU—MÉDAILLE d'OR—PARIS*.

Because of the style of her clothes and accessories, a voice box, plus the wrist joints, she should date around 1885.

The voice box is in her left side. Pull one of the two strings, each with a black glass bead, and Thelma says *Mamá*. Pull the other string and she says *Papá*. There really is a difference in the sound of these words. *Papá* is shorter and snappier. Chummy, *n'est-ce pas?*

Contents of Thelma-Marie's Trunks

2 pr. high button leather shoes
3 pr. slippers—one marked *Jumeau*
12 pr. sox—short silk, lace, cotton, long wool
7 purses—all kinds
2 pr. leather gloves (they fit, too)
3 fans
5 hankies
2 silk ribbon garters
6 tiny hat pins
1 wash cloth—fringed
2 sheets
2 pillow slips
2 toys

11 assorted bonnets and hats— chic!
1 maroon sateen ruffled parasol
1 pegnoir—cotton border-print— adorable!
3 nighties—white cotton
1 flannel underskirt
2 pantywaists
1 winter undershirt
6 panties—plain and fancy
4 cotton underskirts—much lace and embroidery
1 cotton print play dress
2 white cotton dresses—lace and embroidery

THELMA-MARIE

2 silk sachet bags

1 ivory challis dress, pink flowered (see photograph)

1 soft robin's-egg-blue fine wool dress—tailored

1 ivory silk dress—full gathered yoke clear around—gathered wrists—very full skirt and yards of narrow old ivory ribbon in bows with long loops

2 short ivory flannel jackets

1 green wool sweater

1 ivory, tan and blue plaid short jacket with silk bound peplums

1 light blue and ivory striped flannel coat—heavy ecru lace collar and cuffs—ribbon belt tied in front—2 ribbon pompoms on the back

1 bright robin's-egg-blue wool cape—velvet yoke

1 exquisite velvet bonnet to match, trimmed with daintiest silk lace, wide silk dotted ribbon and shower of tiny pink French buds and roses—luscious! (see photograph)

1 ermine tippet and muff

1 larger muff and matching lap robe of lamb's wool

1 beautiful hand crocheted wool afghan with long knotted fringe—made in the muted tones matching the rest of her wardrobe—alternating blue and beige four inch strips—each strip cross-stitched with sprays of bright flowers. Overall size 21 by 36. Comfy!

1 old china commode set—bowl, pitcher, soap dish and soap, tooth brush dish, chamber and waste bucket

1 all bisque doll—barely 1¼ inches high—jointed at shoulder and hips. Painted hair and eyes—dressed in blue silk

1 blue silk and net lined toilet article basket (like one pictured in 1869 *Godey's Lady's Book*) fitted with two hair brushes, one comb, clothes brush, mirror with handle (all of bone), powder box with wee wool puff, and tiniest button hook

1 silver curling iron in silver case

More jewelry than I have, including coral necklace and earrings, tiny rosary, and wee round locket with two tiny pictures inside

Darling old French sewing box with 2 thimbles, tiniest needles, eye glasses that fit, wee scissors, penknife, and beeswax with a one-inch china doll sticking out

Various quaint boxes and baskets to hold all the goodies

2 old wooden doll trunks—very large, with trays (one covered) and rounded tops. These were made in this country. French trunks not shipped here with doll. Too bad!

See: Elizabeth A. Coleman. *Dolls—Makers and Marks*, pp. 37–42.
  Luella T. Hart. *Complete French Doll Directory*, p. 47.

"Decisions, Decisions, Decisions"   THELMA-MARIE

Lionel
Blond Bisque Kestner (?)—25 Inch

Lionel, who is all "gussied up" in a dark blue velvet Fauntleroy suit with separate white shirt, makes a striking figure on his skin horse from Germany. This lovely new pony, although smaller, is the kind of rocking horse I wanted as a child.

In my scrapbook is a page from an old children's book first published in 1912. On it there are two photographs of a small boy with a pony just like Lionel's. Same head carving—same eyes—right front leg lifted at exactly the same angle—back leg placement like his, too. Even the mane and tail, bridle, saddle and stirrups are identical. Apparently, they are using the same molds and patterns today. There are large, detachable rockers for him, too, as always.

How long the real photographs were made before being published is anyone's guess. Lionel and I were very happy when we found this pony in a local department store three Christmases ago.

Lionel's bisque shoulderhead, turned slightly to the right, is almost parian-like in quality. He must have come from a new mold as his blond hair has deep convolutions and his closed mouth, nose and chin with dimple are very well defined. Set-in eyes are brown.

Kestner surely made his stocky white kid body, with its distinctive riveted joints at hip and knee. However, only the glue from the label remains on his manly chest! His chubby legs and feet are of composition —upper arms of kid with a gusset at the elbow. Below the elbow is joined his lower arm and hand of good quality bisque, nicely made and highlighted with delicate pink. He wears long black ribbed cotton stockings and black patent leather oxfords with brown uppers and laces.

Lionel's only remaining marking is on the lower back of his shoulder plate: *1304 Germany N:11.*—his date is probably between 1891 and 1896.

This little gentleman has now joined the blond bisque girls in the collection of Mrs. Margaret Wright of Sherman Oaks, California.

See: "Kestner Dolls" by Bullard and Callicot in *Spinning Wheel*, December, 1959.
Elizabeth A. Coleman. *Dolls—Makers and Marks*, pp. 43, 44.

LIONEL

LIONEL

GENEVIÈVE

Geneviève
Bébé Jumeau—22 Inch

T<small>HIS</small> little girl has *Déposé E 10 J* incised on back of her neck. Her bisque head has lovely modeling and is delicately tinted, nostrils and inner eye corners, too. The mouth is closed; applied pierced ears. Beautiful brown eyes are blown glass, stationary.

Her very dark brown human hair wig is new—from Paris (cork cap). The head, which moves freely, is fastened to a papier-mâché body by a strong hook anchored in a block of wood. This body, fully jointed except for wrists, is strung with elastic cord. Hands are rather large, fingers and thumbs thick. On the small of her back stamped in dark blue ink is:

JUMEAU
Médaille D'or
Paris

This label, coupled with the unjointed wrists, the type of hands and fingers, date her about 1879.

Geneviève wears a ruby colored cotton-backed velvet suit with an ecru lace vest—recently tailored in Paris—but in the fashion of the 1870's. A large ruby velvet ribbon bow sits *atop* the pleated fullness in back. Black lace socks and leather slippers are *her* age, and French.

Geneviève had ten long stiff curls and I divided each one, making twenty bouncy curls—more suitable for a little girl. The first two curls on each side of the face are pinned shorter—giving her a softer, more child-like expression. The double band of narrow velvet ribbon in her hair is taupe; just couldn't match the lovely ruby shade of her velvet suit.

Geneviève is gentle with her all-bisque dollies. Dolores, standing on the chest, is a chubby child, with blond curls from my granddaughters. She is a reproduction by Ruby Sligh, of Glendale, Calif. Dolores is 9½ inches; jointed hips and shoulders and has painted blue eyes. Her white organdy dress, trimmed with lace and featherstitching, has a pink sash. Her bonnet is hand crocheted.

Bye-Lo baby, held by Geneviève, is described elsewhere.

See: Nina S. Davies. *The Jumeau Doll Story.*
     Clara H. Fawcett, *Dolls, a Guide for Collectors*, pp. 58–60.
     Elizabeth A. Coleman. *Dolls—Makers and Marks*, pp. 37–42.

DOLORES, BYE-LO AND GENEVIÈVE

"I Love Little Pussy"   GENEVIÈVE

BETTINA

Bettina

Parian Bisque Lady—13 Inch

Bettina's molded golden hair is short, wavy, and fits her head in back like a little cap exposing just the lower half of her ears. There are tiny ringlets around her face—one quite far down her forehead. Her delicately modeled parian bisque is very smooth and only faintly flesh tinted. Cheeks are pale pink, set-in large blown glass eyes bright blue, mouth closed, nostrils and eye corners tinted. Black lashes and light brown eyebrows are painted.

The shoulderplate has two sew holes, one center front, the other center back. Her lower arms and legs are bisque. She has darling molded high tan boots with heels, four black straps and black side gussets.

Bettina's body is of unbleached cotton, very old, jointed at shoulders and stitch-jointed at hips and knees. Her small-waisted body and upper and lower legs (hair stuffed) are long in proportion to her head.

Her lovely taffeta frock is very old, perhaps original. The very full skirt has the tiniest gray and gold stripes. Black and gold silk braid follows the hemline around the skirt; there are touches of braid at the lace line on the sleeves; a small bow at the jacket waist, in front.

The jacket, of rose and green flowered pin-striped taffeta, has a generous peplum. Low neckline and cuffs are trimmed with ecru silk lace; large sleeve puffs of skirt material. Dainty pantalettes are edged with narrow lace; linen petticoat of real eyelet embroidery, scalloped on the edge.

Bettina is German but unmarked. This lack of mark plus the heels could date her in the late 1860's or early 1870's.

The Chinese chair seems made for Bettina. She looks so relaxed and comfortable. Well, so would we all if we had her beauty, lovely clothes and nothing to do.

See: Eleanor St. George. *Old Dolls*, Chapter VII.

ELIZABETH AND ANDRÉ

Elizabeth
Jumeau Mechanical Music Box—12 Inch (doll)

Eᴌɪᴢᴀʙᴇᴛʜ stands on an olive-green velvet-covered music box, 6½ inches square and 4 inches high, including knob feet. *DÉPOSÉ–TÊTE JUMEAU–2* is stamped in red ink under her black human hair wig (cork cap). She has curly bangs and a mass of bouncy curls, shoulder length. Her rosy little face has large deep blue eyes (blown glass, stationary) and unusually long painted lashes. She has a smooth bisque head, fine modeling, closed mouth, pierced ears, dimpled chin.

Her body, legs and feet are made of unusually hard brown papier-mâché. The upper arms (wrapped) are of heavy wire which enters the bisque forearm at the elbow, ending in a small hook in the palm of each hand. Her lovely bisque hands with fingers separated are modeled for grasping. She holds a brightly enameled wooden drummer boy in the left hand; in the right, a blue crocheted Teddy bear with ears and tiny facial features. Teddy bear is crocheted over a minute bisque doll, with jointed arms and legs. Each toy is just over an inch tall!

André, the French bisque baby (2¾ inch), is tinted and exquisitely modeled from head to foot. His arms extend forward; hands cupped, palms up, fingers defined. Unjointed legs are apart. He can stand, but he doesn't know it yet! His boyish hair is painted brown; eyes blue, rosebud mouth. He is from Paris, but unmarked—probably made in the 1880's. His long, lace-paneled white dress is handmade.

Elizabeth's new chartreuse velvet suit, with braid-trimmed peplum, is a Paris creation. Down the front of the jacket are two rows of ecru braid and six tiny brass buttons. There are wide lacy ruffles on the sleeves and a double lace ruffle at the neck—lace on her petticoat, showing below her full skirt, and lace trimmed panties. Her straw hat is very old but the only original items of clothing are her black lisle stockings.

While the music box plays an old French tune, Elizabeth turns her head to her right, lowers it and looks down at her baby and rocks him five times while showing him the Teddy bear. Then she raises her head, turns it to the front and lifts her left hand up slowly, showing the drummer boy to André. She lowers that arm, turns her head to the right again, then looks down at André. This time she rocks him six times. Next, she lifts her head, turns it to the front, lifts the drummer up once again, drops her head forward and looks at the Teddy bear. All this repeats over and over again as long as the music plays.

The stop-and-go plunger and keyhole are on the back of the box. No wonder the removable hand-wrought iron key is still around after ninety years or so—it's almost five inches long!

ALICE

Alice

Unmarked French (?) Bisque—13½ Inch

Here's Alice, looking as though she were still down the rabbit hole—a little confused as to who she is! Well, she has nothing on me nor on anyone I have asked, so far.

Her bisque head and shoulderplate, closed mouth and large blown glass gray eyes (stationary)—all look French. The tinting and modeling are lovely. There is a 5/16 inch hole on top of her head into which the wig fits. Her painted brows and lashes are golden brown and so is her almost-straight human hair with bangs.

Alice's well-made kid body has a well-defined rump with three vertical seams in back; sawdust-stuffed, gussets at elbows, hips and knees. Cotton covers the short lower legs and stubby feet. Toes are not defined. Tinted bisque arms and hands are set on below the elbow.

Her little black cotton dress and organdy apron are new and so is her dark blue straw hat trimmed with pink flowers and ribbon. She has long white stockings and black patent leather slippers with cunning buckles.

I have seen one other exactly like her, including the long straight hair and bangs. Anyone know who she *really* is?

Alice now belongs to Mrs. Altha Gray of North Hollywood, California.

YVETTE

Yvette

Bru Jeune—23 Inch

THERE is an intangible something which seems to cling like an aura to certain old dolls. It has nothing to do with looks, condition or price. It's just there. You can feel it when you pick up the doll. I'm sure most of you have felt it—an impression that this doll has been especially loved—or was especially important to someone.

Yvette is such a doll. She is very cuddly and has been diapered and diapered. Safety pins have scratched the kid on her upper legs.

Bru Jne 7 is incised on back of her head and on the left edge of her shoulder front; *N.7* on the right. *DÉPOSÉ* at the bottom of shoulder plate in front. She has a personal marking as well. In faded ink on her back, it says *Bessie—1882 Christmas*. It could be authentic—since Bru in 1879 patented "a kind of doll made of kid." Does this mean kid body, bisque head and forearms as she has? Anyway, except for forearms and hands, Yvette's chubby body is all white kid—including stitched toes. The gusset at the seat still works fine—the knee gussets have filled somewhat with sawdust and her legs look slightly froggy.

Her bisque is beautiful and so are her big brown eyes which are blown glass and stationary. Unusually dark shading around her eyes gives her a soft expression. The open-closed mouth shows four tiny teeth molded in the bisque. The tinting of her face and hands is exceptionally nice. There are dots of color in the nostrils and in the corners of the eyes, near the nose. Ears are applied and pierced. The golden brown wig is French, new, and of human hair (cork cap). Her pretty bisque forearms join the kid arm just below the elbow curve.

Yvette's white tucked pinafore and underskirt are French—with almost invisible machine stitching and tiny, tiny round 3-hole buttons. The white bonnet is trimmed with French pleating and lace and has a pale pink satin bow on top and at the back of her neck. She has lacy white French stockings and her black kid shoes have *Bru Jne Paris* stamp-pressed on the sole.

See: Elizabeth A. Coleman. *Dolls—Makers and Marks*, pp. 8–10.
    Luella T. Hart. *Complete French Doll Directory*, p. 100.

ADELE

Adele

Parian Bisque Lady—14½ Inch

THIS regal young lady, who wears her black molded comb like a tiara, is a beauty. Her set-in brown eyes are very large and full-orbed yet have a lovely soft expression. The pretty mouth is closed. Her modeling and coloring are exquisite. Adele's face and neck are flesh color, her beautiful upswept hairdo is blond. The Dresden-type pleated ruffle around her neck and down the front is white, with tiny blue lines and gold beading effect. The rest of her shoulder-plate is perfectly white and smooth. She has pearl eardrops on a gold chain and wears a lovely old star brooch. It fastens the neck of her brown panne velvet bodice with the huge puffed sleeves.

Adele's original brown kid hands and arms, muslin body and red striped lower legs are horse hair stuffed. Her black leather shoes with heels have always been fastened to the legs. She is stitch-jointed at hip and knee.

Adele's unmentionables should be mentioned. They are dainty, lacy, embroidered, ruffled, and be-ribboned. This is true of many dolls but the difference here is proportion. Everything is scaled to her small size and hand done with almost invisible stitches. Such patience!

You should see the rest of her lovely gown. The skirt is ivory satin with vertical gold pinstripes. The overskirt, long, full, pointed in front, is of beautiful, filmy, beige silk lace. There is a long full train of the brown panne velvet falling from the bodice, beginning at the side-front. All the velvet is edged in tiny blue and gold ribbon braid.

Adele's only marking is on her shoulderplate in back *144-4*. She is an early one, her date of the late Sixties or early Seventies.

This fine parian is from the collection of Mrs. Milo Hill of Pacoima, California.

See: Eleanor St. George. *Old Dolls*, Chapter VII.

Campbell Kid
Horsman—12 Inch

Last autumn, the Jumeau girls put on a "Charity Benefit" (masquerade ball and entertainment). Everyone turned out, including some Hollywood stars and it was a huge success. The society columnist was there with photographer in tow. Pictures are on the next few pages.

Elizabeth was refreshment chairman. She promptly enlisted the catering services of the famous Campbell Kid, complete with blue suit and white chef's cap and apron. He was assisted by the bricklaying pig whose culinary fame stems from his best known concoction—wolf soup!

The Campbell Kid is unmarked but made by Horsman (tagged) of fine quality composition—jointed at neck, shoulders and hips. His little fat fingers are outspread; white socks and black shoes molded.

His face is charming—much like the original Grace G. Drayton design used for over 60 years in Campbell Soup advertisements. His painted black eyes look to the right. He has a friendly smile, closed mouth, fat cheeks and molded brown hair. Knees and elbows tinted and dimpled.

The 1912 Campbell Kids had composition heads but not as smooth and glossy. The Kids have also been made in cloth, rubber, plastic and soft vinyl. *American Home Magazine* had an article and pictures of the Campbell Kids in October, 1954. *Life Magazine* had an eight-page spread at the same time called "The Campbell Soup Kids Are Going Places" showing toys, yardage, decals, games, clothing, wall plaques, books and other items decorated with Campbell Kids. Dolls in these articles were cloth bodied (17½ inch with painted vinyl faces) and smaller all rubber squeeze dolls. This fine composition one is earlier—made in the late 1940's.

CAMPBELL KID, ELIZABETH AND
THE THIRD LITTLE PIG

The Third Little Pig
Madame Alexander—11 Inch

THE Third Little Pig, who has changed vocations, is dressed in his original bricklaying clothes—white cotton cap with bill, long red jersey pants with shoulder straps and a striped long sleeved "T" shirt. Cute!

He is smooth composition jointed at hips, shoulders and neck; barefooted, dimpled and tinted at knees and elbows—rosy cheeked.

His head is very clever, with up-standing ears—snout with red nostril dots; wide smile, closed mouth. His painted eyes with vertical ovals and black pupils show surprise. Embossed on his back is *Madame Alexander*. His date, around 1934.

He and the capable caterer now belong to Mrs. Helen Long of Van Nuys, Calif.

TERRI LEE AND TERRI LEE (Colored)

Terri and Jerri Lee

Terri Lee Doll Co.—16½ Inch

Terri Lee, who wore her official Campfire Girl uniform to the Benefit Ball, presented flowers to the entertainers. Here are flowers for colored Terri Lee, whose dancing of the Hula enchanted everyone.

These Terries are made of hard plastic—almost indestructible, jointed at hip, shoulders and neck. Fingers and toes defined, separate thumbs.

The Campfire Girl's hair (Raysheen) is auburn—a softly curled long bob—center part with curly bangs. Her large painted eyes are black, mouth closed, cheeks dimpled.

Terri wears a white cotton blouse and dark blue cotton gabardine skirt. The Campfire insignia is on her skirt pocket and blue wool "beanie." Her tie is red and she wears brown and white saddle shoes and white socks. TERRI LEE is embossed across her shoulders. She was patented November 30, 1948, #528824.

Colored Terri is somewhat different, not just her color—her personality, too. She seems modest and shy in her grass skirt, green flowered print bra and brief shorts. Perhaps it's her bare feet; or her eyes and brows, which are painted differently. Eyes look to the left. She wears bright red paper leis, one around her neck, a narrower one in her hair. Oh yes, her hair—the oddest wig I ever saw—is a very coarse synthetic material, stiff and shiny, but curled and quite effective. TERRI LEE— PAT. PENDING is embossed on her shoulders—her date *before* 1948.

Jerri won boy's first prize for his costume. Since he was not the only one dressed authentically western from stem to stern, it must have been his pony who cinched the prize. None of the other cowboys bothered to bring a steed!

The dark blue demin outfit suits Jerri well. His hat is pressed felt with a yellow silk cord. Belts and holster are embossed leather. High brown boots with white designs and stitching are imitation leather but good looking.

Jerri has a platinum blond wig of tightly curled lamb's wool, soft and silky to the touch. See Terri's description for further details. They are actually the same doll—just different wigs and clothing. All outfits are original.

See: Doll Collectors of America. *Doll Collectors Manual, 1956–1957*, p. 117.
Max von Boehn. *Dolls and Puppets*. Supplement by Luella Hart, pp. 449–451.

JERRI LEE

Sonja Henie
Madame Alexander—18 Inch

Sonja Henie is really a good sport. We looked for her backstage at the Benefit Ball and found her bending over putting on her white shoe skates. She looked up, gave us a big smile and here you see the result! She looked lovely that night in her new full circle white felt skirt, pale pink hand knit sweater and cap (trimmed with tiny blue bead flowers) and white silk high-necked blouse, lace trimmed. Oh yes, there are matching mittens, too, but one cannot lace shoes wearing mittens.

The Madame Alexander Doll Co. presented Sonja in 1939. She is of composition, well modeled and embossed on back of the neck *MADAME ALEXANDER—SONJA HENIE.* A slender doll, she is jointed at neck, shoulders and hips. Her thumbs are separate, fingers joined except tips. Cheeks, elbows and knees are tinted.

Sonja belonged to my late daughter-in-law in childhood. My granddaughters inherited this doll along with about three dozen others, mostly Nancy Ann Storybook and Vogue Ginny Dolls. These, combined with their own dollies (two of everything, you know) make up a collection almost larger than mine!

Back to Sonja. Her little face is pretty, dimpled, eye-shadowed and smiling; open mouth, six teeth. Her brown eyes with hair lashes sleep, and her blond real-hair shoulder-length wig is still curly and in good condition in spite of all the good times she has had with little girls.

I'll let you in on a secret—Sonja alone, of all the dolls at this house, wears a panty girdle!

Sonja lives with Janet Ellen and Gail Lee Corwin of Arleta, Calif.

See: Max von Boehn. *Dolls and Puppets.* Supplement by Luella T. Hart, p. 450.

SONJA HENIE

DEANNA DURBIN

Deanna Durbin
Ideal Doll—21 Inch

Deanna's real human hair is utterly lovely—soft brown with golden highlights and dressed to perfection. The small natural-looking waves start at the center part and continue down to the neckline evolving into shoulder ringlets. Small graceful dips and ringlets curve around her face.

Deanna sang at the Benefit Ball, her lovely voice filling the ballroom, thrilling them all. "CALIFOR-NI-A" and all the rest!

She wore a beautiful new pale blue nylon dress covered with myriads of tiny white forget-me-nots. It was gathered full at the waist, with puffed sleeves, and had a wide neckline trimmed with tiny puffs of white net. White net formed a bouffant overskirt caught up with blue bows in lace medallions at intervals around the hemline. Golden sandals shod her bare feet.

Deanna is of nice quality composition, well modeled, proportioned, and tinted. Sleeping eyes are hazel with brown lashes and shading above. Her mouth is open in a singing-smile, showing six teeth and red felt tongue.

A slender doll, she is jointed at neck, hips and shoulders and has bright red fingernails. Fingers are joined except at tips, thumbs separate.

Deanna was introduced by Ideal Doll Co. in 1938. This one now sings for Mrs. Phyllis Roberts of Reseda, California.

CLAIRE

Claire

Valentine Ballerina—19½ Inch

CLAIRE was "Première Danseuse" at the Charity Ball. The reason for including her in this book is her excellent modeling and extreme flexibility. She is unbreakable plastic, with head and arms of vinyl. Jointed at neck, shoulders, torso, hips, knees and ankles, her body is so well designed that she is truly a lovely doll. Her head is pretty, but not on a par with the rest of her, I think. Her arms and hands (with separate fingers, painted nails) are well proportioned, too. She's fun to play with because of all those joints and her cute clothes. She came in her own suitcase with extra clothing—a gold and white striped formal, a pink transparent negligee, capri pants and topper, etc., all quite well made of nylon. She has high heel slippers and nylon hose.

For the program, Claire wore a net tutu, nylon tights and ballet slippers—all pink. Her rooted golden hair, cut short and curled around her face, was adorned with lovely pink velvet leaves on either side. Her blue eyes have long lashes, and sleep. Her mouth is closed, lips very red; cheeks, bright pink.

Claire is marked at the base of her neck, but I can't quite make it out. However, she was brought out in 1955, by the Valentine Doll Co. of New York.

When my granddaughters read this, they will know for the first time that Claire now belongs to them.

"Ladies and Gentlemen . . . !"   PIERRETTE, PEPPY
AND BARKER

Clowns
5 Inch—10 Inch—10 Inch (seated)

CLOWNS are cosmopolitan, timeless, appreciated by all. These were a big hit at the Jumeau girl's Benefit Ball where they circulated through the crowd with their antics, delighting everyone.

Peppy, the smallest, is full of beans, figuratively and literally. You might know he just came from Disneyland!

Barker was made in Japan. He's an old "M. C." from 'way back—1958, that is.

Pierrette is the real reason for this picture. She was imported from France, I believe, in 1924. At that time, the large music store where I worked ordered some special holiday merchandise around Christmas time. We sold many of them dressed in various color combinations. If I remember correctly, she once had a tag, but it's gone now.

Pierrette's lovely suit is an exact copy of her original, of China silk, midnight blue and bright red. Pointed cap is red, trimmed with a blue ruffle. Midnight blue trousers are long and loose fitting. The coat-like blue jacket has long sleeves. All four cuffs, three large buttons, hem of jacket and wide double neck ruffle, are red. Really a very attractive outfit.

Pierrette is made on a wire armature, and sits permanently on a small square of heavy cardboard hidden inside her clothes. Her long legs are crossed below the knee and she sits safely and charmingly on the edge of cabinets, pianos, tables or what-have-you? Her turned shoulderhead (complete with bust) and forearms are made of white plaster, but extremely well modeled for an inexpensive doll. The balance of her body is wound with some kind of cotton wadding. Her face is truly beautiful, painting is done right, black patches and all. Head is a solid dome—expecting always to have her cap on, which she does. Lower legs and black painted shoes with oxford-type heels are modeled in plaster, also.

I seem to remember Pierrette once had a musical instrument of the string variety, but it is gone now, and so far, have not been able to replace it. But maybe someday, somewhere . . .

Barker now belongs to Master Michael Tuttle of Arleta, California.

ANNE SHIRLEY

Anne Shirley
Effanbee—21 Inch

"A<small>N</small>' the Gobble-uns'll git you——"

Anne Shirley's juvenile readings at the Benefit Ball were excellent and well received. They were made more real by some of the "props" she brought with her. She told the story of the Gingerbread Boy in an amusing way and read a poem about the Billiken, too (composition, 4 inch, 1909, Horsman).

Anne was dressed as a child in a simple pink cotton dress, trimmed with a bit of lace, a pink bow and two brass buttons. Her shoes are pink, socks white.

Her original human hair is golden, quite coarse, yet it curls around her shoulders. It is center-parted, caught back at the temples with pink barrettes.

Anne is all composition, jointed at neck, shoulders and hips. Her face is quite pretty but sober with gray sleep-eyes, real lashes, closed mouth. Between her shoulders is embossed *EFFANBEE—ANNE SHIRLEY*. A distinguishing characteristic of this doll is her very large hands—fingers long and separated.

She represents the actress Dawn O'Day who changed her name to Anne Shirley after her success in "Anne of Green Gables." This doll was first produced in 1935 by Effanbee (Fleischaker and Baum) of New York. The Anne Shirley dolls were sold dressed and undressed until about 1948.

BYE-LO AND SHIRLEY TEMPLE

Shirley Temple
Ideal Doll (Modern)—15 Inch

Shirley Temple entertained at the Charity Masquerade. In her white hand-tailored navy uniform and hat, she sang "Early Bird," then sang and danced "At the Codfish Ball" from the picture "Captain January," bringing down the house!

This Shirley is vinyl with washable golden Saran hair. Marketed in 1958 by Ideal Toy Corp. of New York, she is marked on back of the neck and between the shoulders *IDEAL DOLL S T 15 N.* Jointed at neck, shoulders and hips, she has hazel sleeping eyes, lashes, dimples, open mouth and four teeth. The modeling is well done, the coloring lovely, but I think the first Shirley, also by Ideal, looked more like the real child, don't you?

Shirley has white rayon socks and white plastic shoes. Her black sailor tie was made from an official one. Correctly tied, too!

Bye-Lo Baby
Grace S. Putnam—All Bisque—3 Inch (seated)

This is my favorite Bye-Lo Baby— so wee and yet so perfect. The shape of the head, the bisque, the modeling and delicate tinting are excellent. He has joints at shoulders and hips; curved arms and legs with tiny fingers and toes defined. This Bye-Lo is a Kestner, as were all the tiny bisque ones. There is a worn Kestner chest label, and on his back is incised *20–10* and *Copr. by Grace S. Putnam.* His blue eyes are painted, nostrils tipped, mouth closed.

This infant has the loveliest white christening dress of fine cotton, silk-like in texture. It is long, with minute tucks, lace insertion and lace flounces on the petticoat as well as the dress. Under all that lusciousness is a plain gertrude with a wide band at the top. The dress yoke has several rows of fine shirring and lace edging. Long sleeves have lace edging, too. You can barely make out the hand stitching.

The Bye-Lo, copyrighted in 1923 by Grace S. Putnam, was patented by Geo. Borgfeldt and Co. of New York on January 24, 1925, #208,558.

See: "The Bye-Lo Doll" by Luella T. Hart in *Toy Trader*, February, 1953.

MA AND WILLIE

Willie

Superior (?) Papier-Mâché—24 Inch

In spite of his long legs, Willie likes to sit on Ma's lap just before supper. He's only about eight, you see.

He could be a Superior (like his Ma) with a lost label. The painting and modeling of his face and head, and the feathering of his eyebrows is like the Superior's. His body seems homemade; is stuffed with hay, covered with thin loosely woven cotton material, then recovered, also with cotton material. He is jointed at shoulders, hips and knees; hands of tan leather, toes undefined. Like Ma, he has two sew holes.

Willie's molded hair is black, short and curly, with ears exposed. He has Ma's brown eyes. Wonder if he resembles his Pa at all?

This little boy's clothes are homemade. His smock-like blouse has long sleeves and a white round collar. It is a quaint old gray cotton print with checks of brown and black. "Very serviceable," Ma says. She made brown sateen trousers, also, to wear with the blouse. He has long black cotton stockings and black shoes.

Superior or not, Willie's date would probably be around the late 1870's since the development of childlike faces had come about by then.

Willie's wooden horse is labeled on the bottom,

McLaren-Sleight Corporation
A-B-C Toys are
BUILDERS OF HAPPINESS
Made in the U.S.A.
Niles,   Michigan.

Dobbin sports a leather saddle and red saddle blanket. As you can see, Willie loves him very much.

These fine old primitives and accessories are from the collection of Mrs. Muriel Rahmn of Sherman Oaks, California.

See: "M & S Superior" in *Doll Talk*, March–April, 1963.

Ma

M & S Superior—31 Inch

Ma is a neat-haired, fresh-aproned type of mother with a placid demeanor. She is a typical Superior—label on back of papier-mâché shoulderplate reads *M & S Superior—2015.* Little is known about this type of doll. Some with different initials or numbers said *Made in Germany* so perhaps she was too, but, to my knowledge, so far there is no proof.

Ma has large painted brown eyes and a molded Civil War hairdo—center part, black scallops outlining the face and a double row of vertical sausage curls around the back from ear to ear.

Her body, made of strong unbleached material, is old and machine stitched. Jointed at hips, shoulders, elbows and knees, with tan leather forearms and hands; hair stuffed; this body could be commercial. Toes are stitch-defined, shoulders have two sew holes back and front.

Ma's pink and white flowered black calico print is two-piece. Blouse has long sleeves, and is rather full, gathered at the neck with a draw-string. Skirt is very full, gathered on to a band. Her freshly-starched apron, with gathered bib, is pretty pink calico with tiny red and white lines, old and quaint. Clothes could be original except for white kid shoes with heels which are newer.

CHIEF MIGHTY HUNTER

Chief Mighty Hunter
Armand Marseille Indian—9½ Inch

THIS little copper-colored guy looks worried. There are two vertical wrinkles above his nose, between the eyebrows. Combined with his large deep brown piercing eyes (glass and with no pupils) he *does* have a concerned expression. It makes me think of something I read recently about American Indians. The article stated that from childhood, the eldest son of the chief was taught to frown, to develop wrinkles and an expression of fatherly concern for his tribe when he, in turn, became chief. True or not; known by A & M or not, this doll looks full of responsibility. This is not the result of an accident to the bisque in the greenware stage. I have seen several other A & M Indian dolls—all with this same modeling. The wrinkles were planned.

Mighty Hunter was a pretty sad Indian at first. He had a shirt of dirty doeskin and delapidated brown leather trousers. A red and white polka-dot rag tied around his head bristled with parrot feathers, bunched together like a toddler's bouquet. The pants were discarded, shirt cleaned and turned back for front and new trousers fashioned of copper-colored suede. I was amazed to find at least two dozen colorful feathers in the bunch, enough to make a full headdress reaching to his heels! With his matching bright red, yellow, green and black beads, he's all set up for business! He now has doeskin moccasins, bead trimmed, as befits a great chief! Also, he has a bow and arrow so he won't starve to death. His decorated headdress has long strips of leather, beads, and two brass buttons (from my housecoat) like pictures in the Indian books. "Real chic" or "Heap ugh" or whatever an Indian would say!

Mighty Hunter's swivel neck bisque head is quite cleverly modeled for what was an inexpensive doll in the first place—advertised as a premium doll first in 1895. His redskin coloring, both head and body, is perfect and his face definitely looks Indian even when considered without headdress or clothing. His high-bridged nose is different from that of the average doll. Mouth is open showing four teeth; nostrils and eye corners dotted. Long black mohair braids hanging down over each ear are plaited and tied with red yarn. Incised on back of his head is Germany—A M 5/0. Hunter's composition body is a bit on the crude side but fairly well proportioned and jointed at hips and shoulders.

"Happy hunting, little redskin!"

See: Evelyn, Elizabeth and Dorothy Coleman. *The Age of Dolls*, p. 120.

Baby Gladys
J. D. Kestner—17½ Inch

GLADYS' white kid body is like the one Kestner patented—riveted at knee and hip—with adorable stitched toes. It is sawdust packed, and well designed. Bisque arms with tinted hands are joined just below elbow gusset.

The bisque head has Kestner quality—modeling, tinting and careful painting. Color dots in nostrils and eye corners; nice mouth, four teeth. Original silver-blond wig is mohair; sleeping eyes sky blue.

Incised at the top of her head in back, is *Dep-F-150*. Under the kid across the bottom of her shoulderplate is *Made in Germany* with the type of capital G with curlicues on the upper part so much used on early Kestners.

Her dress is toddler-type, circa 1900—white barred dimity, with lots of fine lace and insertion, and an extremely full wide ruffle on the yoke extending all the way to the back. It has a high neck and long sleeves with insertion on cuffs and neckband. There are old black tie slippers and lavender cotton stockings to match the hair ribbon and bow on her chest.

Gladys is held by Penelope—one of a set of Kestner twins like the first twins in the book—except for dark wigs, *two* open mouths and clothing. Penelope and her twin, Prudence, have beautiful outfits made of apricot-colored imported cotton—shawl collars and bonnets trimmed with heavy lace. Ribbons on bonnets are periwinkle blue.

Gladys, Penelope and Prudence date in the early 1890's.

These Kestner twins are now in the collection of Mrs. Stephen Salatich of Reseda, California.

Gladys has a new home with Mrs. Paul L. Wood of Sepulveda, California.

See: Elizabeth A. Coleman. *Dolls—Makers and Marks*, pp. 43, 44.

GLADYS AND PENELOPE

Chuckie
Chase Stockinet—14 Inch

THIS is Chuckie's favorite play place —a bit sloppy under foot but fun for frogs, dogs, boats and bare toes. I tried to catch this rascal off guard and get a *candid* shot but he was too smart.

His sober little face is well modeled for a cloth doll and quite nicely painted, in oils. He has blue eyes, closed mouth, eye and nostril dots, brown lashes, pink cheeks, golden hair; eyebrows to match.

This doll is the older type, since his pink sateen body is not waterproofed. In going over Chase research material, I do not find complete agreement on the actual date of commercial launching of the play doll. However, they do seem to agree on the early part of the 1890 decade. He was made by Mrs. Martha Jenks Chase of Pawtucket, Rhode Island.

Chuckie's head, shoulderplate, arms and legs, are of stockinet material (cotton stuffed) first sized, then painted with three coats of waterproof paint. He is stitch-jointed at shoulders, elbows, hips and knees; thumbs and ears separately applied. Fingers appear to be separated but actually are not. They are stitched; roundly and solidly stuffed; thoroughly painted and pink tipped. Toes are treated in the same manner.

I'm sure Chuckie is, or was, marked. However, two covers have been sewn over the original sateen torso and I haven't ripped them off to see.

This child would wear his blue-trimmed sailor blouse and dark blue denims to bed if we'd let him and frequently does—nap time—hat and all!

Chuckie belongs to Mrs. Paul L. Wood of Sepulveda, California.

See: Janet Pagter Johl. *Fascinating Story of Dolls*, pp. 144–146.
Eleanor St. George. *Dolls of Three Centuries*, pp. 104–106.
"Chase Stockinet Dolls" by Clara H. Fawcett in *Hobbies*, October, 1962.

Timmy
Minerva Tinhead—13 Inch

I'M glad Timmy can't read! He is rather plain and ordinary looking, like so many of the tinheads at the turn of the century. He could be an *early* Minerva. The gray Steiff elephant dates a bit later—1912 according to an old magazine ad—but could be earlier also.

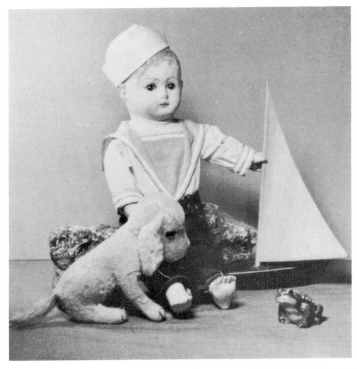

CHUCKIE

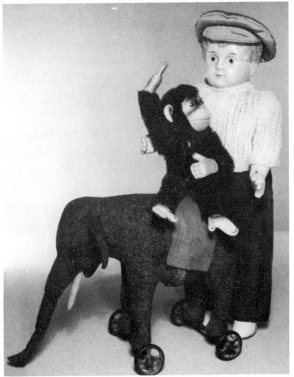

TIMMY

Tim is blond with a boy's hair styling. His painted eyes are blue, eyebrows brown. He has eye and nostril dots and a red line above the eyelids. The mouth is closed; two sew holes on back and chest.

Embossed on back of the shoulder is *Germany*; on the chest *MINERVA*, with a helmet underneath. Minerva heads were first made about 1894. In 1901, the Minerva trademark was registered here by the importers, A. Vischer & Co. Montgomery Ward carried them as late as 1936.

Timmy is jointed at shoulders and hips. His torso is unbleached cotton, excelsior stuffed. Arms and legs are composition, shoes and socks molded and painted an odd ivory color not matching the flesh pink of his head at all. The unmarked body may have been manufactured here. Most metal heads were imported without bodies. He is well proportioned and in nice condition—unusual for a tinhead.

He wears one piece knit underwear, dark blue bib corduroys, and a hand-knit ivory-colored wool sweater. Jip, the Steiff monkey, has been trying to talk Timmy out of his new blue cap, but I don't think he'll go for that!

See: "Metal Dolls Had Their Brief Play" in *Doll Talk*, May–June 1960.
Gladys Reid Holton. *A Monograph on Metal Doll Heads.*

Amy
Rag Doll—14 Inch

Here's Amy who has just triumphantly toddled over to the chair to get the toy horse. She almost didn't make it. It was her first try, and now she has a real feeling of accomplishment—very necessary for small fry!

The little folding carpet chair is child size and old, about 1885. The name *Hattie* is painted in gold on the top wood panel above the carpeting. The dapple-gray horse with brown glass eyes and the baby, too, are of the early 1900's.

Amy is another of those dolls who seem to have a special aura about them; a feeling that she was mighty important to someone and greatly loved. One of her little cloth hands with stitched fingers has been sucked!

Anyway, she's important to me in her little white calico print with

AMY

tiny black lines and dots. Red featherstitching around waist, neck and cuffs. This quaint old dress is not original, but it could have been. Her under things are white and plain.

Amy's body is machine made of unbleached cotton material, cotton stuffed. It is very simple and could have been made at home. Her head, however, is commercially made, probably in the early 1900's. Her face is sweetly painted (or printed) with blue eyes, long lashes, nice eyebrows, nose, closed mouth, and rosy cheeks. Even the inner eye corners are tinted red, very realistically! Her painted hair is brown and she wears a red hair ribbon.

Somewhere, during my childhood there was such a doll, with exactly the same face. Was it a playmate's doll or was it my own? I once had a *china* doll I no longer remember . . . There's *something* about Amy's little face . . .

Grandma
China Shoulderhead—30 Inch

GRANDMA, as this pretty black-haired china is called, is very young appearing in spite of her hundred years or more. She is a delicate pink cast, with large blue eyes and very rosy cheeks. She has a red line above her eyelids, a deep bust, three sew holes and sloping shoulders, all signs of an old chinahead. Her white line center part and high-sided hairdo, with its shelf of vertical curls running around the back, is mid-nineteenth century style, too.

The body of this nice old chinahead is new unbleached muslin, well proportioned. The torso is sawdust stuffed, the limbs filled with kapok. She is stitch-jointed at hips, knees and shoulders.

Grandma's lower legs are blue-and-white striped cotton material, and high black cotton heelless boots permanently cover her shapely extremities.

The picture does not do justice to her lovely frock. Bright pink roses and tiny star-like white blossoms spill profusely over the full gored black skirt and closely fitted, long sleeved waist. Four narrow pink satin ribbon bands are stitched around the skirt at four inch intervals giving the effect of separate flounces. Two rows of beautiful wide handmade lace decorate the waist, collar and cuffs. There is a pink satin bow at her throat and a lovely pink-on-black cameo.

One afternoon I asked her about the lovely white shawl. She took off her glasses, laid down her knitting and was retrieving her ball of red yarn when I noticed her beautiful arms and hands for the first time. I was fascinated by her long, tapering, graceful fingers; the prettiest I have seen on a china. Whether her arms are as old as the head, is anybody's guess. They are definitely old German arms, but they do not show the normal play wear as does her head. Could be, though, that Grandma has always been a lady of leisure, means and maids. This could account for her youthful appearance, too, as well as her lovely hands. Incised on the inside of the elbow is #3, the only marking on the entire doll.

Grandma and the child's rocker, circa 1910, are from the collection of Mrs. Roy Cowdrey Sr. of Panorama City, California.

GRANDMA

ROSALEE

Rosalee

Unmarked German Bisque Shoulderhead—15½ Inch

A DIGNIFIED German lady is Rosalee, with a sober expression and conservative hair arrangement in new auburn mohair.

Rosalee's beautiful medium blue chiffon velvet gown, with bustle effect and train in back, is just right for her—age-wise too. She is probably of the late 70's or early 80's. Her original bulbous bisque legs with molded white ribbed stockings and high heeled, high strapped black boots, help to date her. She has #4 on back of her turned-head bisque shoulderplate.

The tinting on Rosalee's cheeks is extraordinarily bright, and the high coloring extends up to the eyes, almost to the temples and across to the ears. There are inner eye corner and nostril dots, a black eyelash line and a red line above *that*, as in many old chinaheads. Eyelids and eyeballs are molded. Eyebrows are true auburn, the only ones I've seen.

Her painted eyes are darker than sky blue but very bright and intense. She has a pretty closed mouth, perfect little nose, full cheeks and little round chin, with fullness underneath. Her neck is rather short and full—shoulders sloping—pierced ears with pearl drops.

Rosalee's bisque arms and hands are original, too. Backs of hands are tinted and hands are quite turned back at the wrists. Fingers are defined, thumbs separate. She came on her original body but it was fit only to pattern a new one. She is stitch-jointed at hips and knees.

Let's go back to Rosalee's pretty dress. It is high waisted with low neck and full sleeves to the elbows. Lovely ivory lace flounces reach almost to her wrists. Crystal beaded net scallops make a "V" to the waist and the over-skirt effect in the front is caught up by beaded net. Three rows of the same ivory lace are fulled onto her white satin petticoat below. The blue velvet skirt is edged with lovely silk ribbon braid.

This lady has gorgeous old white undies—layers of them! Do you suppose she is blushing because they were mentioned?

This unusual doll was shown at the Bowers Museum in Santa Ana, California. She is the property of Mrs. Pat Schoonmaker of North Hollywood, California.

Christine

Unmarked German Bisque—34 Inch

C HRISSY is handy with the younger children and loves to push Yvette's carriage.

Christine's head is smooth tinted bisque; dimple in chin, dots ·in nostrils and inner eye corners. She is a very pretty little girl with a reddish-brown naturally curly ventilated wig and big brown sleeping eyes with lashes. Incised on back of her head is *1001—6½ Germany*. Her date—probably before World War I.

Christine's well constructed composition body is fully ball jointed, with nice hands and feet. Toes are defined and dimpled. She wears real child's white kid slippers and white cotton socks. Her long white cotton dress and dainty pinafore were borrowed from my granddaughters. Bonnet is white silk with lace and pink satin ribbon.

In "Story Hour" you can see Christine really works well with children. Is Lionel teacher's pet—he's the only boy—or is it Yvette, the French Bru baby? To Chrissy's right are the golden-haired Kestner twins, Patience and Humility; Nannette with long tresses; Jennifer in pink, and Prudence, the dark-haired Kestner twin—minus bonnet. There's Margaret again with a daisy in her hair and Penelope, the other dark-haired twin. (All described elsewhere.)

Yvette's 1874 wooden wheeled wicker carriage was made by Ludlow Toy and Manufacturing Co. of Ludlow, Vt.

Christine is now in the collection of Mrs. Helen Long, of Van Nuys, California.

See: Eleanor St. George. *Dolls of Three Centuries*, p. 189.

CHRISTINE AND YVETTE

"Story Hour"

ARABELLA

Arabella

China Shoulderhead—19 Inch

ARABELLA is very old now, probably a good 110 years or more, and still pretty. Her head has a soft pink cast, quite rosy cheeks, pink nostrils and eye corners, red eyelid lines, and blue eyes with white highlights. Her black hair has a white line center part, comes down smoothly to the ear tops and has even, vertical, neck-length curls all around the back. Shoulders slope and there are three sew holes—back and front—no marks.

Her body is stuffed with horsehair. Arms are brown leather, fingers stitched; legs of red and white candy-striped material. Her heelless black boots, sewn on, are very worn but still have the original brass buttons—two each. She is stitch-jointed at hip, knee and shoulder.

Arabella's original "covered wagon" clothes are plain but handmade. Her faded red calico print dress has white pearl buttons down the back, all the same size but each with a different design and very pretty designs they are, too. This is often found on old doll clothes. Wonder if it was the style for buttons at one time? Who knows?

Arabella now belongs to Miss Arax Arklin of Granada Hills, California.

See: Janet Pagter Johl. *More About Dolls*, p. 123.

"Tea and Talk"　　ARABELLA, HATTIE AND
BROWN-EYED SUSAN

Hattie
China Shoulderhead—20 Inch

Hattie's blond serenity is a nice foil for the black-haired girls in the group. She is a turned-head with blue eyes, rosy cheeks and slight double chin. Hair is center-parted and waved in rows to just below the ears.

Hattie's ruffled dress is apricot organdy—a luscious color for one so fair. The velvet bow and sash are brown. Her new unbleached muslin body is well designed, jointed at shoulders, hips and knees. Lower legs have horizontal brown and white stripes; beige kid boots have heels. Wire from under the shoulderplate down into the old china hands enables them to stay in position.

This chinahead may be old; no marks—not even size marks, which began about 1860. The red line above each eye may indicate age, also.

Hattie now belongs to Mrs. Helen Long of Van Nuys, California.

Brown-Eyed Susan
China Shoulderhead—19 Inch

Susan has a child's hairdo of the 1880's but it would be sweet on a little girl of today; shiny, well kept, black bobbed hair with wavy bangs and much fluffyness in back. There are brushmarks at her ears and on her forehead. Her painting is quality, too, including red dots and lines in the proper places. Her large brown eyes are highlighted; little mouth is perfect.

Susan's sawdust-stuffed body is heavy unbleached muslin, slightly stained with the passage of time, but still firm. It is stitch-jointed at shoulders, hips and knees. There are two sew holes on her shoulder-plate, back and front, but no markings.

Something happened to Susan's old china arms and legs; the ones she has now are excellent replacements. The calves of her legs are the real chubby kind, with blue bows at the knees, and hightop brown boots with small heels.

When Susan came to live with us she had on a very beautiful skirt and jacket, but it didn't suit her at all. It was made for a grown lady. Was she ever thrilled when we went to the "Dolly's Dress Shoppe" and let her buy what *she* liked! She chose a pretty little red print, calico type, trimmed with lots of black braid. It runs all around the hem of her very full skirt, around the neck, waist and sleeves. There is a deep "V" of braid and three tiny buttons on her chest. The lower part of the sleeves is a full organdy puff, lace trimmed. Her lace-edged white panties show a bit, giving that old-fashioned look. Oh yes, there is a little black straw bonnet lined and ruffled with the dress material and further decorated with black shiny feathers and small white daisies but she carries it—I just can't keep a hat on that child!

If you care to look, there is a picture of her in grownup clothes on page 151 of Eleanor St. George's book, *Old Dolls*. She is on the left.

See: Clara H. Fawcett. *Dolls—A Guide for Collectors*, Chapter V.

Fanchon

Bru Jeune—20 Inch

THIS utterly feminine French child is a charmer. She captivates all who know her, even her dollies. It isn't just her beauty; there's an air of sweetness about her and a softness—perhaps that's it,—softness!

Fanchon's large blue eyes (blown glass—set) are full-orbed and very expressive with unusually large irises and pupils. Her smooth bisque head is delicately modeled and tinted with open-closed mouth, chin dimple and pierced ears. Inner eye corners and nostrils are dotted. The swivel-neck head is attached to the bisque shoulderplate with a heavy spring. Her original silver-blond mohair (cork cap) has wavy bangs and falls in little soft curls about her shoulders. Incised on back of the neck, and on each side of her shoulderplate in back, is *BRU Jne 7*. There are small high breasts molded in the bisque.

Her slender body and limbs are made of a combination of materials; jointed at neck, shoulders, hips and knees. The upper arms and thighs are metal shafts, kid covered. The ball and socket shoulder joint is so constructed that the arm swivels easily in a full circle and can also move in toward or out from the body. Her beautiful bisque forearms and dimpled hands and elbows are pink tinted at finger joints, knuckles and nail lines. The hand-carved lower legs and feet are wooden with well defined toes.

The drawing clearly shows the thigh and hip mechanism. The hardwood post extends up inside the body almost to the breast plate. The torso, packed with very fine fibrous material, perhaps marsh grass or moss, is covered with fine quality heavy kid which extends down over the thighs.

Theoretically, this type of Bru can sit, as the hip is jointed. However, I believe none of them could *ever* sit straight up on the floor like most jointed dolls. Mine can sit in a reclining position or be forced *nearly* straight up if securely tied that way, in a chair. There are two reasons why this is so. First, the metal shaft was not cut out enough in front to allow a stuffed abdomen to assume a true right angle to the thighs. Secondly, the kid over the rump is not cut quite full enough to stretch that far.

On Fanchon's chest is an old paper label which reads:

BÉBÉ BRU Bté   S.G.D.G.
Tout Contrefacteur sera saisi et poursuivi
conformement a la Loi.

FANCHON WITH TESSA, BITSY, MAUDIE
AND BEULAH (seated)

Translated:

BÉBÉ BRU *Patented*   *Without Guarantee of Government.*
All imitators will be seized and prosecuted in
conformance with the law.

I do not know the exact date for Fanchon, but around 1880 would be pretty close.

Fanchon's old pink silk taffeta dress has frilly flounces of dotted silk net, ivory in color. The skirt is very full with wide pleats at sides and back. The ruffled bustle, in back, holds the skirt out 1880-style. The five-inch net flounce on the skirt is decorated with tiny bows of pink ribbon, as are the shoulders, sleeves and belt. Featherstitching runs around the hem, cuffs, belt, neck and down the yoke, back and front. Tiny pink pearls outline the neck. Pink silk stockings and old French slippers of black leather complete her outfit. Shoe soles are stamped C.M.; brown rosettes cover the toes.

Large letters of the alphabet, printed in color on paper, have been applied to the seat and back of the little old chair. It was made long ago, probably in the 1880's or early 1890's, and once had rockers. Fanchon's dollies, Tessa, Bitsy, Maudie (on arm) and Beulah (seated) are described elsewhere.

See: "The Wedding of the Brus" by Thelma Miller in *Hobbies*, June, 1962.
"The Lovely Bru Children" by Alberta Fulton in *Toy Trader*, June and October, 1962.

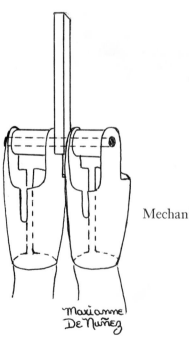

Mechanism for Bru Legs

Marianne
De Nuñez

"I Have a Little Shadow—"   FANCHON

"Love Letter?"

Marianne
Parian—7¼ Inch

MARIANNE is a joy, so tiny and perfect, with bisque so smooth she is fun to feel. She sits in her little gold chair trying to digest the contents of her letter. Disturbed, she does what most gals would do—throws herself on the bed for a good cry!

The old hand-carved slat bed and little lady are about the same age—from the late 1860's. So are the handmade silk patchwork quilt (feather-stitched in variation), muslin sheets, mattress and lace-edged pillow slip.

Marianne's only marking is 5 on back of her shoulderplate. Her faint skin tinting escapes notice unless compared with the white bisque arms.

"Woe Is Me"

Her small face has been painted with precision; cheeks pink, eyes a bright blue, mouth closed. Her light golden hairdo has a center part; scallops edge her brow to eye level, then become two rows of tiny vertical sausage curls from side to side, around the back. This is fun to feel, too, comb marks and curls being well defined. Her pink muslin body is sawdust stuffed, jointed at shoulders and hips. High black two-strap boots are molded and have small heels; fingers are defined but joined.

Marianne's thin white cotton dress is princess style. Pale blue braid and lace ruffles come from the middle of her back, cross her shoulders and run down the full length of the front to the bottom lacy ruffle of the skirt, ending there in blue ribbon bows. The low neck exposes her lovely neck and shoulders. There is a ruffle, braid and lace at the cuffs of long sleeves. Her undies and pantalettes are plain, of soft white cotton.

This outfit is original. When she came, the commercial stiffening was still in her dress and everything was brown with age. Feeling that removable soil adds nothing to a doll, everything was carefully swished in a glass jar of suds and all is nearly white again.

"Feeling better now, Marianne? Hearts really do not break, you know. Dry your tears and we'll have a cup of tea!"

DORIS, SKEEZIX, HERBIE AND TINY TOWN ALICE (on chest)

Doris

J. D. Kestner—14 Inch

D ORIS is getting her doll and toy collection ready for the Girl Scout show. There's Skeezix and Herbie from the comics, and a little Dutch boy with a boat—all made in Germany except Herbie who is from Japan. They are bisque, and Skeezix's head swivels. Alice, with the doll carriage, is a modern doll-house doll made in this country. Her tag says *Tiny Town Dolls—Alice*. The others are modern flexible doll-house dolls imported from Germany.

You will notice Doris is wearing her green Girl Scout uniform, an official one, made by the Terri Lee Doll Co. Her green belt, yellow tie, and brown oxfords are just like the real ones. She is proud to be wearing her first long stockings—nylon. It's fun once in a while to see how an old doll looks in modern clothes.

She's a very old Kestner (before 1896); incised high up on the back of her bisque swivel neck *C—Made in Germany—7*.

Doris has unusually large gray-blue eyes, sleeping; a well shaped nose and tiny open mouth with two teeth. Her coloring is delicate, eye corners and nostrils tinted. Her beautiful fluffy mohair wig is red-blond and unusually nice. She has a typical excellent Kestner fully ball-jointed composition body. Stamped over her right hip in back is the oblong box with the word *Germany* inside and below that, the number 0.

Doris has joined the collection of Mrs. Altha Gray of North Hollywood, California.

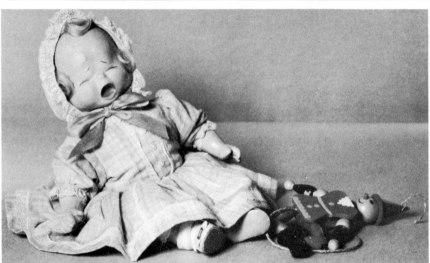

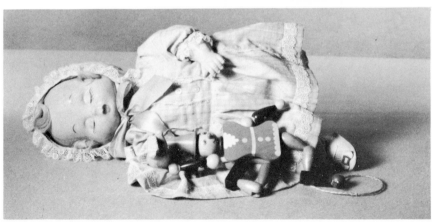

SMILY TRUDY (top) WEEPY TRUDY (center)
SLEEPY TRUDY (bottom)

Trudy
Three-in-One Doll—9 Inch (seated)

Trudy is a flirt. She has charmed the Austrian jumping jack into amusing her with his antics. Now he's standing alone—*standing alone?!*—Oops! There he goes—flat on his back!

"There, there, Trudy, don't cry. It couldn't be that bad. He's not hurt, you know. Let me dry your big blue eyes and we'll pick him up by his cap string and——. Well, bless my soul, honey, I didn't know you were that tired!"

This cunning baby was first patented May 21, 1946 (#495,638), by the Three-in-One Doll Corp., New York, N.Y. There is a flat knob on top her head, protruding through the bonnet, which turns her head to show three separate facial expressions: smiling, crying and sleeping. The head is composition and so are the curved baby arms and legs, but only for a short way above the elbow and knee curves. The remainder is pink muslin, stuffed, and attached with stitch-joints to the soft body. The head is mounted on a vertical shaft. The head and shaft turn freely within a wooden casing inbedded in the soft body of the doll. This casing protrudes about ½ inch above the body, forming the neck. Quite ingenious! Blond curls peek out of the bonnet—actually they are fastened to the bonnet, not the head.

Trudy's smiling face has large painted blue eyes which look to the left, long up-swept painted lashes, a big smile and a cute little button nose. Trudy's crying face has diagonal brows drawn down and close together, eyes squeezed shut and a very large, almost round, open-closed mouth. The sleeping face has a tiny heart-shaped closed mouth, lashes sweeping the cheeks. There are the tiniest red nostril dots imaginable on all three noses!

The little pink, gray and white plaid dress is new, trimmed with fine lace, most of which is laid on flat in the French manner. There are short puffed sleeves, a full skirt, tiny buttons down the front. She has new white slippers, pink and white socks. Her bonnet matches the dress, and is tied with bright pink ribbons. The unusual thing about this bonnet, the white fleece under-bonnet (and the one she wore originally) is that they all have a large buttonhole on top which buttons down over the turning knob.

I have seen two other Trudy's in original clothes. One wore a pink fleecy snow suit with a pointed cap. The other wore a short white cotton dress and bonnet with *Sleepy Trudy, Smily Trudy* and *Weepy Trudy* printed in tiny pastel circles. These word circles resemble flower garlands at first glance. Clever!

"Come, Trudy lamb, you'll be more comfortable in your little bed."

Trudy is from the collection of Mrs. Robert Burckert of Sylmar, California.

See: "U.S. Doll Trademarks 1913–1950" by Luella Hart in *Spinning Wheel*, March, 1956.

Yvonne
French Fashion—13½ Inch

Yvonne is a honey in her ivory satin dress and is all original: golden mohair wig on cork cap, satin shoes matching her dress, three-bead blue earrings included. Oh yes, unmentionables, too. The silk mitts were a later addition.

She has the sweetest expression on her little face. Her modeling is exquisite—parian-like with its paleness and very delicate tinting. Her coiffure is perfect. It is parted down the center with ringlets above each ear. Hanging down her shoulders are seven little long curls, exactly like many pictures in *Peterson's* and *Godey's Lady's Book*, around 1865–1870. This hairdo, her dress with large bustle and long train, and her delicate coloring, all put her clearly within this period.

This little "Poupée Parisienne" has a closed mouth, and blue blown glass eyes, full-orbed, but stationary. Even her tiny nostrils and inner eye corners are tinted. Her swivel-neck head and shoulderplate are of smooth bisque.

Yvonne's white kid body, legs, arms and feet are filled with fine sawdust. She is narrow-waisted, with gussets at the hips, knees and elbows. All ten fingers are separately wired. Incised on the back of her neck is the number 2—her only marking. An early Jumeau? Perhaps—but many firms made "Poupée Parisiennes."

She is now in the collection of Miss Arax Arklin, of Granada Hills, California.

See: Nina S. Davies. *The Jumeau Doll Story.*

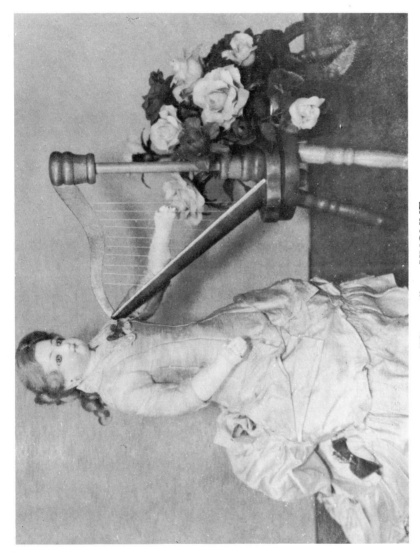

"Concert"   YVONNE

Elmira
Colored French Bisque—5 Inch

You'd look surprised, too, if your infant charge perched himself so nonchalantly at such a tender age! Elmira only took time to remove her shoes and socks.

This little girl with a papier-mâché body has *34-13* incised on back of her socket-head. Her black pupilless eyes are hand blown, stationary. Tiny as she is, she has Negroid features. Her slightly open mouth shows a white pearly substance indicating teeth. Ears are nice and her modeling is well done for a small dolly.

Elmira's bisque is dark chocolate color—but unlike most colored bisques, it is colored clear through, not tinted.

Elmira is fully ball jointed including wrists. Wee hands have separate thumbs, fingers well defined; tiny toes, legs and feet are just darling. Wig is fine fuzzy wool of some kind. Peaked black eyebrows give her a surprised, bright-eyed look.

About her origin and date—she seems old, perhaps a doll-house doll of the 80's—and quite Frenchy looking. The body construction is French. The hip sockets have the back ledge at the base of the buttocks, a French characteristic, and the feet and legs are of the same type as many the French model.

Elmira's brown and red flower print cotton dress is very simple and old. A plain waist, gathered skirt, high neck and long sleeves, with panties and bonnet to match, somehow look cute on her. The bonnet is French type, peaked at the back with long ties of the same material.

Back to that new turtle-marked celluloid curve-legged baby, before he tumbles. They're still coming over from Germany. In the nursery where he lives is his pal—a flesh colored celluloid. Cute as buttons, the two of them. Jointed shoulders and hips—2½ inches, seated.

"Grab him, Elmira, and put on his diaper!"

Having written this—I am now in love with Elmira but it won't do me any good. She belongs to Mrs. Pat Schoonmaker of North Hollywood, California.

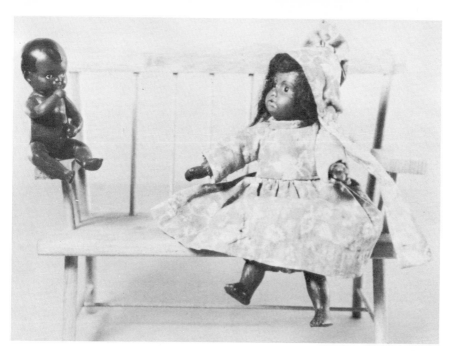

ELMIRA

"FREELOADERS" AND ANGELA

Rosalie
French (?) All Bisque—11½ Inch

BUTTON, button, who has the button?" That's what they are playing at the party, and guess who really *has* the button tightly clenched in her tiny fist? That's right, Rosalie.

This child of the Eighties certainly looks like a Parisian, although I'm not sure she is. The exquisiteness of her modeling and tinting plus the high quality of the bisque makes one think of the old French dolls. There are no markings. The swivel-neck head has some sort of plaster composition dome, her mouth is closed and her big brown eyes sleep. There are dots in corners of eyes and nostrils.

The flanges of her shoulder and hip joints are lined with kid. The knees, elbows and feet are dimpled, little toes well defined—dimples all over her toddler body, as a matter of fact.

Her beautiful maroon satin redingote-type frock is new, very Frenchy and all handmade. The dress is of white silk and batiste, with a lace overskirt. There is smocking on the dress in front and on the coat at the waist, in back. The large round collar, cuffs and low waisted belt are all trimmed with Val lace. The maroon points on her short skirt are piped in tiny white silk braid.

Rosalie's golden curls, of fine human hair, are capped by a white china silk bonnet, lacy and be-ruffled. A perky maroon bow sits right on top, another under her chin.

Long white silk stockings and handmade high white kid boots with buckles and bows complete her outfit, and cute she is, too.

"Come now, Rosalie, let go of the button so we can go on with the game!"

Rosalie is from the collection of Mrs. Ellery C. Thorpe of Glendale, California.

ROSALIE

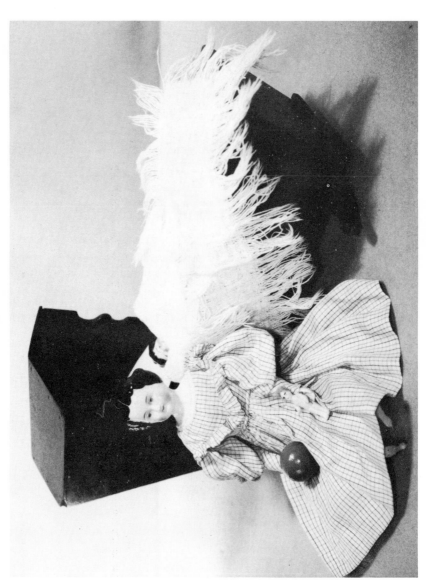

TOTTIE

Tottie

China Shoulderhead—11 Inch

HERE's an old-fashioned child with a modern frustration. There's a new baby in the old cradle and while that could be upsetting in itself for a small girl, that isn't what bothers Tottie. Every morning, Tottie runs to the cradle with a doll and toy only to find out, all over again, that sister just isn't big enough to play. Today she sat down beside the cradle with a serious expression on her sweet little face to try to figure things out. Hope she comes up with an answer!

Tottie has a story that goes with her and dates her as having been purchased about 1875 for a little girl adopted from an orphanage.

Tottie's china is very white and clear, cheeks softly tinted, eyes blue. Her black hairdo is like Grandma's and she, too, has the red eye line, and deep sloping shoulders. However, her china legs with black boots and heels place her later than Grandma, and so the above story could be authentic. Tottie's cloth body is sawdust stuffed and jointed at hip, shoulders and elbows. Her old china hands and arms as well as her head and feet show normal wear from play over the years.

Tottie's adorable little soft tie-silk dress is white, cross-barred with tiny black, blue and gray lines. The style is about 1834 with lacy white pantalettes to the boot tops, leg-o'-mutton sleeves, high waist with large square collar (ruffle trimmed) and long gathered skirt, calf length.

She's a darling size, feels compact in one's hand and has a quaint facial expression—her lids are heavy with sleep. I have lost my heart to this china child!

Tottie and the quaint old cradle are from the collection of Mrs. Roy Cowdrey, Sr. of Panorama City, California.

"Day Nursery" AMOSANDRA, SARALEE AND GERBER BABY

Amosandra

C.B.S. Colored Baby—7 Inch (seated)

THESE three babies, who are not at all color conscious, are each important people in their own right. Amosandra, the first and smallest, has a coined name from two very well known radio and television stars, Amos and Andy. She was designed to represent the baby daughter of Amos and Ruby of the "Amos 'n' Andy Show" on C.B.S. radio.

This little doll is made of rubber and in raised letters on her back it says: A M O S A N D R A (each letter in a separate box).

©
COLUMBIA BROADCASTING
SYSTEM, INC.
Designed by
RUTH E. NEWTON

She was manufactured by the Barr Rubber Products Co. of Sandusky, Ohio, apparently a supplier to the Gail Novelty Co., the distributors. The C.B.S. copyright was issued on February 28, 1950, #575,751. However, in spite of this date, sales for this little doll were going great guns as early as March, 1949, at least in New York, according to an article by Galen Drake in *Toy Trader* for April, 1949.

Amosandra has curly molded hair painted black, and her rather large painted eyes are brown and look to the left. She is a nursing baby with a hole in the center of her parted lips and came complete with nursing bottle, teething ring, rattle, soap dish, hot water bottle and a "Birth Certificate."

Amosandra has a typical curved arm and leg infant body and is flange-jointed at neck, shoulders and hips. Fingers and toes are well defined and dimpled. Her soft little pink and blue cotton print dress is new. There is a squeaker in her head but such a happy baby rarely squawks!

Little Miss Allison Marsh of Santa Barbara, California, now owns Amosandra.

See: *Toy Trader* for April, 1949.
    "U.S. Doll Trademarks 1913–1950" by Luella Hart in *Spinning Wheel*, May, 1956.

Saralee

Ideal Colored Baby—11 Inch (seated)

S<small>ARALEE</small> is quite a doll—my favorite of the three—a pretty and appealing baby. She seems almost real, and looks for the world like many of the darling colored babies I have seen.

Her appeal is no accident. She was planned that way in 1950 by Sara Lee Creech, to be a source of pride for the children of her own people. Saralee was modeled by the award-winning sculptress Sheila Burlingame from over 1000 photographs of negro children taken by Miss Creech.

Many well qualified people backed the project and Saralee was finally produced by the Ideal Toy Corporation. The box label reads *Ideal's Beautiful Saralee Negro Doll. More Than Just a Doll—An Ambassador of Goodwill*. With her came a full printed sheet giving a detailed account of Saralee from idea conception to production listing the universities, educators, ministers and other important people who were interested in her production and gave their support.

Saralee's head and extremities are made of resilient plastic vinylite. Her molded hair of tight little curls is black. Her eyes are brown with black lashes, and sleep. Her open-closed mouth is adorable, and naturally tinted. There is a faint rose tint on cheeks, too; ears are particularly well modeled.

Her head joins the body with a flange fitting and turns from side to side. The shape of her head, side view, is lovely and the back of her head with its creases and fat rolls is just darling. *C-17-Ideal Doll* is embossed at the base of her neck. The body is brown cotton cloth stuffed with kapok enclosing a crying box. (Who cries?) Her chubby, creased and dimpled arms and legs, curved at elbow and knee, are joined to the cotton body half way between knee and hip—shoulder and elbow. This arrangement makes her soft and flexible. Fingers are separated; toes well modeled.

Saralee's clothes are all original and well designed. Panties and slip are of white cotton—lace edged. Dress is white organdy trimmed with lots of lace and light blue embroidery. It is gathered very full at the waist; tiny sleeves are puffed; bib effect in front with blue satin bow and streamers. There is a matching wide-brimmed bonnet with lace and blue ribbons. Socks are white rayon and white shoes tie with narrow tape.

See: Inez and Marshall McClintock. *Toys in America*, p. 434.

Gerber Baby

Sun Rubber Co.—8½ Inch (seated)

THERE are several magazine ads for the Gerber Baby from 1955 to 1959 in my scrapbook. She was a premium doll, offered at first for 12 Gerber's Baby Food labels or cereal box tops and $2.00 cash. With her came a nursing bottle, four cereal play boxes and a dish and spoon. According to her pictures she also came equipped with diaper and a bib with *GERBER BABY* sewn on or printed.

This doll has a vinyl plastic head with molded light brown painted hair and a distinctive bit of topknot to the left, in front. She has set-in stationary gray-blue eyes, a nursing mouth, three dimples, and a dear little nose.

Her typical curved arm and leg baby body is rubber, flange-jointed at neck, shoulders and hips. Her four fingers are joined and there are cute dimpled feet.

Baby has a new white cotton dress and a pale green hand crocheted sacque. Her squeaker no longer works.

Incised on back of her head is *GERBER BABY* and below that is the circle C and *GERBER PRODUCTS CO.* On her back is *Manufactured by The SUN RUBBER CO., BARBERTON, O., U.S.A. PAT. 2118682 & PAT. 2160739.* Quite a legend for one so small!

MEHITABEL, CHARITY AND HANNAH HAWKS

Charity
Greiner—22½ Inch

Here is blue-eyed Charity and her children on an outing with little Hannah's carriage of the 1860's or early 70's. Mehitabel wanted to push the wooden three-wheeled buggy with the folding hood but couldn't reach the handle! ·

Charity has a label on back of her papier-mâché shoulderplate which reads: *GREINER'S, PATENT DOLL HEADS, #7, Pat. Mar. 20, '58. Ext. '72.*

Charity's body is of white canvas, hair stuffed and seems homemade. It is well proportioned, however, and stitch-jointed at elbows, hips and knees. Her undies and long-sleeved, princess-style buttoned-down-the-front white dress with black dots and interesting black border are old and may be original. Her beige stockings with horizontal tan stripes and her handmade leather shoes, are old and interesting. Arms and hands are brown kid.

Her blond molded hair is center-parted, with puffs and curls around the face. Her closed mouth is a cupid's bow. Nostril and eye corner dots; red eyelid line, too. With her sweet and placid face, she looks like the kind of mother I'd like to have been!

All three dolls and the buggy are from the collection of Mrs. Muriel Rahmn of Sherman Oaks, California.

See: "Ludwig Greiner—Doll Head Maker" by Marion B. Wilson in *Antiques Journal*, October, 1960.

Mehitabel
Pre-Greiner—16 Inch

This unsmiling, solemn-faced child has a typical Pre-Greiner hairdo: center part, exposed ears, sausage curls all around the back. Set-in glass eyes, brown and pupilless. Her twice re-covered, much-patched body is filled with straw. Arms and legs are wooden, hand carved. The lower third of legs and feet is painted light red. She is jointed at hips and shoulders.

Mehitabel is very proud of her pretty new yellow print dress with lace trim and narrow black ribbon bows. The blouse is made separate from the full skirt and has long full sleeves tied at the elbow. There are white pantalettes with wide lace showing below. She is the oldest of the three —probably of the 1840's.

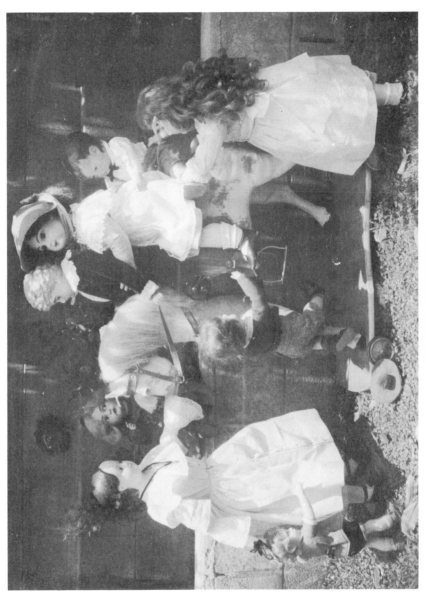

"EAGER BEAVERS"

Hannah Hawks
Greiner—12 Inch

Hannah is a rare one, being so tiny and all. She has been much played with, too, but still has her original brown leather arms and hands and her blue striped lower legs and black leather boots, the tightly sewn-on kind with simulated heels. Her commercial-looking muslin body is stuffed with hair.

Hannah's white dress and undies are loaded with embroidery and tucks. Long sleeves have a large full puff and very wide embroidered cuffs below. Her belt and bow are red silk ribbon.

Hannah has molded black hair, center-parted, with little curled scallops around her face. Short curls fall from the crown to the neck, sides and back.

This little girl has lost her label. However, she is identical with another one of the same size which is still labeled—one way to identify an old dolly.

Eager Beavers

What did I tell you? Look who has grabbed the best seat and the best dressed boy. Gisèle—no less! Looks like she's not about to let go, either. Poor little Fritzie would slide right over the pony's tail if it weren't for Nanette.

Peaceful, who is *much* too old and dignified to ride a pony, holds his bridle, although she knows he's gentle and loves children. Toni is torn between wanting to ride and hiding behind Peaceful's skirts!

Well-mannered little Janet sits in the shade on the wall, quietly waiting her turn. She's just not the "pushy" type.

James, who has shinnied half way up the pony's leg, obviously isn't thinking clearly. Where would he perch if he *did* make it?

COSETTE

Cosette

A.K. French Bisque—9½ Inch

IF I'm in jail for refusing to return this outfit to it's rightful owner, you'll understand, won't you? It wasn't for sale, so you see, I had no choice!

Cosette is the cutest little French doll. The modeling and pale bisque of the socket head are very good. Her serious mouth is closed; enormous eyes set-in and dark brown. Nostrils and eye corners are tinted. Her only markings: A K in script and 13-20 incised on back of her head. Cork cap, light blond mohair wig (long, falling in soft curls below her shoulders), bangs with tiny velvet ribbon tied just above.

She may be all original. Her clothes are old and handmade. Dress is pale blue brocaded sateen, lined with white. Apron is embroidered, scalloped in white, hand-edged in red. There is lace at neck and on puffed sleeves at elbow.

Cosette's body is fully jointed except for elbows. It is all composition except thigh and knee balls which are wooden. Her tiny feet are encased in long thick black stockings and three-button high brown kid boots, the cutest ever! marked on the sole C in a keystone figure. Cosette is well proportioned and "feels good" in your hands.

Cosette's black pony is a nice one. The wooden platform has been painted black and no mark appears. It *may* have had *Germany* underneath like many platformed animals (four iron wheels) at the turn of the century.

The horse and cart look as though they were designed to go together. Note the adequate harness and trappings. The pony is covered with black wool cloth; black glass eyes are pupilless. His handsome tail is horsehair; mane and forelock are rabbit fur.

The wicker basket-cart is varnished a soft tan, matching the harness. The large wheels have metal rims and spokes. This may put the cart in the 20th century. Anyone know for sure? The cart shafts and seat are of varnished wood. In fact, the whole outfit is exquisitely crafted.

Pierre, the cream colored pooch with huge eyes and swivel neck, always gets into the act. Sometimes he runs behind but mostly he rides inside on the floor, draping his chin on the wicker trim!

Cosette and her accessories are from the collection of Mrs. Thelma Bouchey of Toluca Lake, California.

"It's Not Your Turn!"   LOUISE WITH ALICE, DEE DEE,
SUSAN, MARIETTA AND YUM

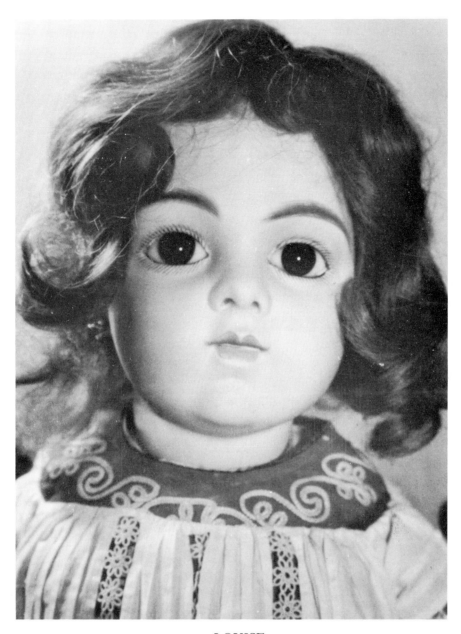

LOUISE

Louise

Bru Jeune—34 Inch

Guess who helps the children, now that Christine has a new home? That's right—Louise. They understand her, in spite of sketchy English. She just came over from Paris, you see—all by herself!

Here she takes Yvette outside with her old toy rattle. The bone handle has a perforated metal sphere on top which jingles. Real baby rattles were made like that, too, in the 1880's. Yum, the Chinese boy, dangles from Louise's hand.

Louise is a love, with fine bisque, closed mouth and enormous blown glass brown eyes. She has inner eye corner and nostril dots. Her auburn hair, softly curling around her delicately tinted face, helps to give her a child-like expression. The naturally curly wig (of human hair) and cork piece are topped by a white wool hand-crocheted cap. Ears have rose-shaped gold earrings. The chin is dimpled; beautiful bisque hands and arms dimpled, too—four on each hand, two large ones at the elbow. This is the type of arm, like Fanchon's, which is hinged to the kid-covered metal shaft and actually extends up into it a short way. The rounded end of the elbow is incised *11—12.*

Her body in its entirety is like that of Fanchon—minus the chest label. Incised on back of her neck is *BRU—Jne. 13;* left edge of her shoulder-plate in back—*Bru—Jne* with *N. 13*—right edge. *Déposé* appears at bottom of shoulderplate in front.

Louise's clothes are all old. Her quaint French red woolen dress hangs from the shoulders and is very full—nice for curtseys. It has pearl buttons clear down the back and is lavishly trimmed with white soutache braid at the neck and sleeves and another band, twice as wide, around the bottom of her skirt. Hand embroidered scallops edge the sleeves and provide the hem, but below the scalloping is a French pleated four inch flounce of the red wool; 1½ inch flounce on cuffs, too. This was a child's dress, a real labor of love. Louise's batiste pinafore is gathered at the waist and neck, trimmed with rows of fine tucks and yards of tatting. Some little girl wore this for Sunday best, I'll bet.

Her black kid slippers have *BRU Jne—PARIS* stamped into the leather sole and the little red socks say *FRANCE.*

Ev'ry little breeze seems to whisper "Louise." . . .

"Responsibility"   YVETTE, LOUISE AND YUM

Yum
Chinese Boy (Modern)—9 Inch

Yum! Now look what you've done! Catch that cricket! He's getting away!"

That Yum! He's a real "ham" at heart. He has all the other children lined up to watch his show. I'll show *him* if he doesn't retrieve that bug! Good luck or not, I'd rather it stayed in the cricket cage, wouldn't you?

Yum is a modern "Chinese." He's cute to have in a collection, though, because so many old children's books from the 1860's on, show children playing with dolls somewhat like Yum. He fits in almost anywhere, with his cute little blue cotton jacket and pants. His features are very well done, embroidered by hand and his fingers are separated and stuffed with cotton, as is his body. The coat is closed in front with blue silk frogs and he wears tiny black shoes just like real Chinese boys and men wear today. His hair is black yarn and his short braided queue sticks straight up! Need I add that he came from China?

Yum's friends on the floor are modern Japanese dolls such as can be found in almost any oriental store now. They are beautifully made, however, if one really takes time to look at them carefully. Their bright red figured kimonos are adorable, too. Traditionally, red is used for baby girls and dark but bright blue for boys in the orient, or so a Chinese acquaintance told me.

"Cricket Mischief"   YUM

The largest baby on the carved Chinese chest is around 25 years old. She is all composition, jointed at neck, shoulders and hips, a regular curved-leg baby, unmarked. I say "she" since her clothes are "pinkish" red satin, trimmed in green ribbon and lots of red and silver braid. Her little jacket is closed at the neck and wrists with tiny pearl beads. The cuffs of her pants and black satin shoes are braid trimmed, too. The matching cap has red pompoms over the ears, and she wears her long black silk hair in a queue down her back. Her head modeling is very nicely done—Chinese in expression—with a dear little nose and rosebud mouth; eyes and eyebrows painted black. Oh yes, the back of her neck has *two* little fat rolls, one of the few times I have seen this on a doll. I would like to know more about this baby. This type was sold in Chinatown, too, and I believe she is American-made.

Notice the startled expression on the face of Yum's little brother, Foo. Maybe he's afraid he'll get the blame. He sometimes does. Yum can run faster!

Monique
F. G. French Bisque—9½ Inch

Thе only original thing about this child is her head. Well, they say to keep your head under all circumstances and this Monique has done. Actually, she was once a mechanical of some kind and a special neck fastening was made to secure her head to this body. Elton Rippel of Upland, California, made her cute new composition body, jointed at shoulders, elbows, hips and knees.

The modeling and tinting of Monique's head are good; bisque smooth, mouth closed, ears pierced. Her large brown stationary eyes are blown glass and have a sober expression. Her red-brown human hair (cork cap) is a long bob and curls up around her cap. There are curly bangs in front.

F. G. in an oval with number 1 underneath is incised on back of her head. She was probably made by Fernand Gautier (or Gaultier) in the 1880's.

Her long-sleeved, low-waisted coat-dress is a soft gray-blue wool. It is trimmed with tiny white braid and silk covered buttons down the front. There is a large self-bow on her rump. Full pleated ivory lace lines the pleats around the bottom. Her cap is chiffon velvet in the same shade of blue, and white rabbit fur makes her muff and trims the cap. Both are lined with rose-pink satin ruffles. Little slippers are black velvet.

See: Elizabeth A. Coleman. *Dolls—Makers and Marks*, pp. 22, 23.
    "French Doll Trade Marks, 1885–1900" by Luella T. Hart in *Spinning Wheel* August, 1957.

DEE DEE, MONIQUE (in chair), MAUDIE, MARIANNE AND
ELEANOR-ROSE

JAMES

Dee Dee
Simon and Halbig—18½ Inch

THIS little auburn-haired beauty with her fluffy bob (mohair replacement), has a real distinctive personality. She's always into mischief, a foot stamper, a born tattletale and yet loveable with it all. It was Dee Dee who got James in trouble the time he jumped up and down on the bed. It was she who nearly tripped Louise the day Louise promised to wheel them in the carriage—if they'd take turns. As you can see from the picture some of the kids just don't "savvy" taking turns!

Dee Dee boasts a fully jointed Jumeau body of papier-mâché. An old round yellow sticker on her back reads *BÉBÉ JUMEAU—Diplôme d'Honneur*. Whether she has always had that body, who knows? She came from Paris and her head probably was one of those special orders the French doll companies imported from Germany to assemble in France.

Her exquisite modeling, the "greasy" looking beautiful smooth bisque, her large stationary blown glass brown eyes and cork cap, all spell age and export. There are four holes ⅜ of an inch in diameter 'way up at the edge of the cork, one above each ear and one over each eye. What for?

Dee Dee's closed mouth is one of the prettiest I have seen, with full lips, two dimples—one in her chin, one just under her lower lip. Her coloring is different and quite lovely. Ears are pierced through the lobes. On back of the head, at the edge of the cork, incised in script, is *S 12 H* and below that, *949*. Eye corners and nostrils are tinted.

Her silk dress is very old, made in Paris but not original. It is a most beautiful shade of rose-pink, long-sleeved, low-waisted, large-collared and pleated from the neck down, box pleated below the belt. Collar and cuffs have ecru lace edging and there is a big bow on her rump, in the manner of the 1880's. She has old black Jumeau slippers with *Paris*, *Déposé* and the winged bee stamped in the sole, and white cotton socks.

Dee Dee holds Maudie, a four inch bisque shoulderhead. Maudie has a pink cotton body, bisque arms and legs, painted black hair, *Germany* incised on shoulderplate. She wears a pink and black print dress with overskirt and white pantalettes.

Dee Dee now belongs to Mrs. Altha Gray of North Hollywood, California and Maudie to Mrs. Helen Long of Van Nuys, California.

See: "Simon & Halbig, Master Craftsmen" by Genevieve Angione in *Spinning Wheel* beginning December, 1962.

James
Schoenhut—17 Inch

James is all boy. He looks pretty proper in the picture with the sand pail but check the one he didn't know I took. Breathes there a boy with soul so dead he never jumped upon his bed?

The kelly-green knit cap and sweater look wonderful with his bobbed red mohair wig. He is nicely modeled with molded eyeballs painted blue, open mouth and four molded teeth. James' wooden head is the conventional type.

This conventional head, modeled by Harry Edison, son of Albert Schoenhut and patented in 1919—according to at least one authority, was on the market as early as June, 1915. In my scrapbook is a large display ad from *Woman's Home Companion* for December, 1915, for "Schoenhut All-Wood Dolls." The main photograph, 12 inches high, shows a conventional type wooden doll with curled mohair wig, molded painted eyes, open-closed mouth with four molded teeth. The body is the early one with steel spring joints and swivel action patented in 1911.

James' light blue shirt has tiny prints in several colors of boys, girls and kittens at play. The short wool pants are tweed; cotton socks, tan; shoes black, with ties.

Stamped in the wood on his shoulder is:

SCHOENHUT DOLL
PAT. JAN. 17 '11. U.S.A.
& FOREIGN COUNTRIES

James now belongs to Mrs. Helen Long of Van Nuys, California.

See: "Schoenhut American Dolls and Toys" by Margaret Whitton in *Toy Trader*, March, 1962.
    "Schoenhut, Wooden Doll Craftsman" by Elizabeth A. Coleman in *Antiques Journal*, June, 1963.

"I'm Telling!"   JAMES AND DEE DEE

"Baby Show" NELLIE, ELIZABETH ANN AND BABY KEN

Elizabeth Ann

J. D. Kestner Baby—11½ Inch (seated)

Elizabeth Ann (center) was my first baby—doll, that is! I saw her in the Goodwill—went dashing to the library—studied doll books three hours—staggered back to the car with ten of them, then dashed back to get her. Fortunately, she was still up for adoption and I proudly took her home. She was the identical bisque baby with molded, tinted hair I had wanted so much in childhood, and in mint condition!

Elizabeth has *J.D.K. 12—Made in Germany* at the base of her neck, in back. Her sleeping eyes are gray-blue and she has real lashes. Her cheeks are rosy, nostrils colored. There are two wee teeth and a little red bisque tongue. The curved-leg composition body is dimpled in the right places and rosy at knees and elbows. Also, her big toes stick up!

Elizabeth's dress and slip are pink organdy; the pale green woven wool sacque was my grandson's.

I'm not sure of her date, but I first fell in love with one of her sisters about 1915.

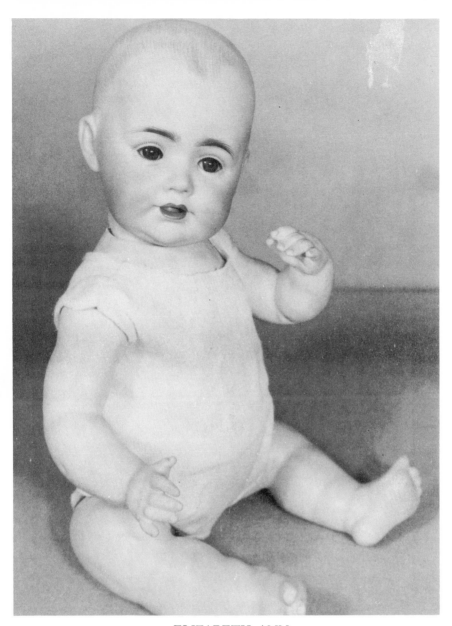

ELIZABETH ANN

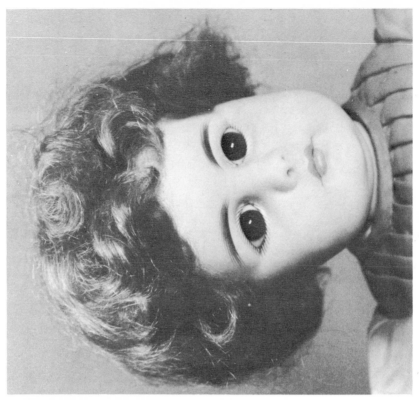

DEE DEE

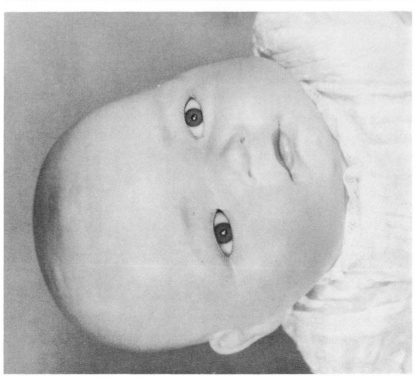

BABY KEN

Nellie

Kämmer and Reinhardt Baby—11½ Inch (seated)

Nellie (left), before 1891(?), has K & R in a six-pointed star and *Simon Halbig 36* all incised in the bisque on the back of her pretty little head. Her curved-legged composition body is very chubby and the knees are rosy tinted and dimpled. Her large gray eyes sleep and she has two teeth.

Nellie has a dimple in each cheek and tinted nostrils. Her eyes look as though she once had lashes. Her baby cap (wig) is soft brown and new.

She wears a real new-born baby's white organdy christening dress—with yards of lace and dainty embroidery—all handmade in Portugal.

Nellie is now in the collection of Mrs. G. W. Carter of Los Angeles, California.

Baby Ken

Century Baby—11 Inch (seated)

This little "sober-sides" (right) represents a younger baby than the other two. Actually, it is another example of the effort to compete with the Bye-Lo Baby. Personally, I like him better. Ken is a truly lovely baby—the rosy tinted head, anyway. He has a broad face, sleeping blue eyes—wee baby nose with nostrils tinted and adorable closed mouth. The molded hair is tinted soft brown, with faint eyebrows to match. He has two dimples—chin and under lip.

The bisque is fine quality. Incised on back of the flange neck is *Century Doll Co. Kestner—Germany*. The Century Doll Co., an American firm, was started in 1914 by Max Scheurer and his sons Bert and Harold. However their "Century Baby" was made for them by J. D. Kestner in Germany. The date for Ken, of course, shortly after the Bye-Lo Baby.

Ken's body is disappointing, although original. The fat little composition hands—with dimpled fingers outspread—are darling, but the arms are much too short. The entire body is of muslin—stuffed with gray cotton wadding—but it is rather wide and flat and too short, as are the legs.

Ken came in his original white dress—coarse cotton with lacy ruffle part way down the front. I saved it, but dressed him in a 1905 family christening dress, slip and flannel skirt. His ivory silk cap is very old and is laced with blue ribbons. He's all boy, and much cuter, in his new-old clothes.

See: *Playthings*, January, 1964, p. 75.

Fritzie
Käthe Kruse—17 Inch

Тнıѕ obliging toddler looks like a real child. His head is molded canvas—hand painted in oils. He has brown hair and well modeled ears, pink tinted. The eyes are his most realistic feature; blue and perfect, highlights and all.

His sturdy, chunky body is flesh-colored cotton material, tightly packed with a fibrous substance, almost as fine as hair. He is jointed at hips and shoulders, has stitched fat fingers and toes, thumbs applied separately.

Fritzie can stand alone. The soles of his little feet are reinforced inside with heavy cardboard. One sole is stamped *Kathe Kruse 20204* and the other *GERMANY*. He is an early one, made shortly after 1912.

His clothes are copies of originals—short pink pants, long sleeved white shirt with round collar and black bow tie. White socks and shoes are new.

See: Janet Pagter Johl. *Your Dolls and Mine*, pp. 88–90.
    Luella Hart. *Directory of German Dolls*, p 5.

FRITZIE AND TONI

Toni

Lenci—13 Inch

Toni's face and features are so well molded and realistically painted, that he photographs like a live child. His wavy bobbed hair looks girlish, but he's a boy and as full of mischief as his Steiff teddy bear!

Toni's head, arms and legs are of flesh-colored felt, his body of durable cotton material; flesh-colored, excelsior-stuffed. He is jointed at hips, shoulders and neck. His lovely large brown eyes, which look to the side, are framed above with long brown lashes and below with a soft gray line. The natural-looking wig is golden mohair, and there's a dimple in his chin.

All of Toni's clothes are felt, too, including blue shoes, with the exception of undies and white-ribbed cotton socks. He has a cute medium-blue jacket with short sleeves, white collar and cuffs, two tiny pockets and six black felt buttons down the front. The little short pants are black, with blue cuffs piped in white.

Toni's toes are stitched; fingers separate and outspread, except the third and fourth, which are stitched together.

The Lenci dolls were made in Italy by Scavini, who began making dolls about 1914. They were patented in Turin, Italy, September 8, 1921. The later ones were made of pressed cloth. Toni, of course, is an early one.

See: Clara H. Fawcett. *Dolls, A New Guide for Collectors,* pp. 187–189.

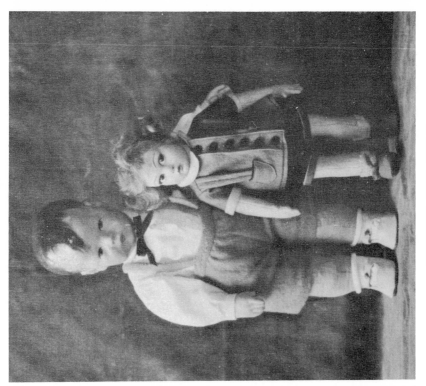

FRITZIE AND TONI

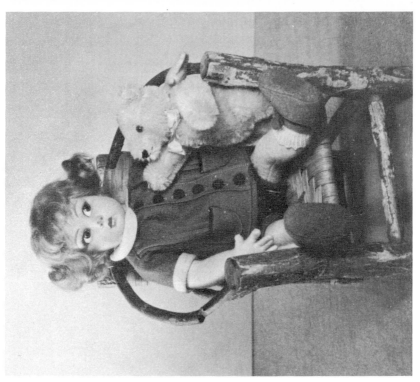

TONI

Scootles

Rose O'Neill—15 Inch

Tea, anybody?"

Scootles stands stark naked before me as I write—what a cute baby! She is all composition, jointed at neck, hips and shoulders. Short molded hair is painted light brown. She has a big smile with closed lips, big brown painted eyes, rosy cheeks and wide pudgy nose. Her fingers are all separate, spread out widely like the Kewpies, only more so! Scootles has fat rolls on the inner side of the upper legs, dimpled knees and a big dimple for a belly button! She is the "Baby Tourist" from the Kewpie stories, as you know.

Scootles' friends are German bisque Kewpies. The single ones are incised *O'NEILL* on the feet. The largest one has a Rose O'Neill sticker on the back as well. The "Lovers" have nothing—except each other. Must have lost their label while their heads were in the clouds! Scootles has the barest remnants of faint embossing on the bottom of her right foot. She was first produced around 1930 by Cameo Doll Co., Port Allegany, Pennsylvania.

The china tea set, my pride and joy, is marked, too. On the bottom of the teapot it says *ROSE O'NEILL—KEWPIE—GERMANY* in her familiar script.

"Thanks, Scootles, don't mind if I do!"

See: Maude M. Horine. *Memories of Rose O'Neill,* revised edition, 1954.
    Ruth S. Freeman. *Encyclopaedia of American Dolls,* p. 27.
    Rowena Godding Ruggles. *The One Rose,* Chapter XI.

"Tea, Anybody?"
SCOOTLES

MIMI AND LILI-CHÉRIE

LILI-CHÉRIE

Lili-Chérie

F. G. French Bisque—15 Inch

THIS candid shot shows Lili-Chérie packing the trunk for Rubyette's trip. Each of the girls donated something to make the trunk complete and the trip a success. Lili's donation: her favorite hairbrush. The old trunk has been in our family almost a hundred years. The sturdy little old Bentwood chair has the original caning and was made by Michael Thonet.

Lili-Chérie's head is smooth bisque, softly tinted. The mouth is closed, chin dimpled, cheeks quite full, a characteristic of this type of F. G. Her full-blown brown eyes are lovely; inner eye corner and nostrils dotted; ears pierced. Her cork cap is topped by a long, slightly curled brown human hair wig, quite Frenchy looking.

This pretty head is on a Jumeau body and probably always was, since so many are found that way. The papier-mâché body, with old type solid wrists, is jointed at neck, shoulders, hips and knees. The feet are wooden; toes defined.

Lili has an old French dress of dark red wool. It is pleated from the neck to the low waistline, front and back, has a flared skirt and long sleeves. Old ivory lace trims the neck, cuffs, waistline and skirt. Her shoes are old, handmade, of grayish suede leather; stockings made from crocheted gloves.

Incised on back of Lili's neck is *F.G.G.* The back of her body is stamped in blue ink, *JUMEAU—Médaille d'or—PARIS.* She was made by Fernand Gautier (or Gaultier) probably in the early 1880's.

Lili-Chérie is now in the collection of Miss Arax Arklin of Granada Hills, California.

See: Elizabeth A. Coleman. *Dolls—Makers and Marks*, pp. 22, 23.
    "French Doll Trade Marks, 1885–1900" by Luella T. Hart in *Spinning Wheel*, August, 1957.

RUBYETTE

Rubyette
Bru Jeune—19 Inch

THIS brave little French child waits for the train with her trunk, lunch basket, parasol, purse and bird cage. The birdies are a gift for *grand'mère*.

Lovely Rubyette is like Fanchon in every way except size, wig, and clothes. Ruby, too, has her original wig but it is an angora goat cap, over cork, rather short and fluffy, wind-blown, you could say, and platinum in color. Her short coat, muff and little bonnet are platinum, too, made of teddy bear cloth—very popular the first decade or so of this century. Cuffs are trimmed with lambskin. Pastel yarn flowers trim her little cap.

Rubyette's red serge dress is trimmed with black velvet ribbon. It is high-waisted and full-skirted with self-ruffles from waist front to waist back, across each shoulder; suitable for traveling and looks well with her coat. Her socks are white cotton net; pierced ears have solid gold earrings.

She is incised *Bru Jne 9* on back of her neck and *Bru Jne* on the left shoulder blade—bisque shoulderplate, that is! On the right blade is N.8.T. Her red leather slippers have *BRU Jne—Paris* stamped into the sole.

"Porter, *help* this child who travels alone!"

RUBYETTE (Photo by K. L. Corwin, Jr.)

"Peek-a-Boo!"   JENNIFER

Julie
Kämmer & Reinhardt Baby—10 Inch (seated)

Tʜɪs beautiful pale bisque baby—so proudly shown off by Jennifer—is very old. Her only marking is **K. & R.** in a six-pointed star, incised on back of her head. Absence of the word *Germany* could date her before 1891; and her history bears this out.

Julie was a two-family doll. One family of girls outgrew her and gave her to the Julie for whom she was named. Julie's mother made her white sweater and blue booties. The knit undershirt and panties, with button crotch, came with her, long ago. She is all original including her silver-blond baby cap of mohair. Her mouth is open, showing bisque tongue and two tiny teeth; color dots in eye corners and nostrils. Her composition baby body is nicely modeled and dimpled.

Her gray eyes have a lovely soft expression and something added. In the eye mechanism is a slide latch. If Julie is laid down on her right side first and *then* flat—she stays wide awake. If just put down flat, or turned to the left—she immediately sleeps. Humans should have an arrangement like that!

Oh yes, the bonnet. She had to have one because sister did. We found this white lacy French one and then Julie smiled for the birdie!

Jennifer
Heubach Köppelsdorf—21½ Inch

Jᴇɴɴɪꜰᴇʀ has a real big smile and laughing brown eyes—a happy child. She was made in Germany, or so it says on back of her head, along with *Heubach Köppelsdorf 300-2*. Her fully jointed composition body is unmarked. Jennifer's new red-brown wig is mohair; sleeping eyes have long lashes. Cheeks are rosy; bisque of high quality.

The little cap and dress are two piece pink organdy, quite new—one reason she wanted her picture taken.

Jennifer has reached the primping stage. She doesn't really use face powder though—she's just pretending.

This pretty little girl, being a character doll, probably appeared around 1915.

Jennifer now baby sits for Mrs. Stephen Salatich of Reseda, California.

JULIE AND JENNIFER

Nanette
Armand Marseille—25 Inch

NANETTE's lovely face, as pale and delicately tinted as a cameo, is a fine argument for collecting German bisques. The texture of the bisque is almost silky with careful modeling; dimple, too. Her large sleeping eyes are blue-gray with real hair lashes; mouth open, four teeth. Her ash-blond luxuriant mohair reaches her waist.

Nanette's fully jointed composition body is beautifully designed, with dimples on the knees and feet. There are little soft indentations where the chubbiness shows, from neck to toes, back and front. Notice her hands—larger than most German bisques—and more life-like.

Her dress is be-ruffled pink organdy, the full skirt falling in soft folds. Socks are pale pink; white satin slippers. The plum colored parasol of ruffled sateen gives a little French accent; it's Thelma Marie's.

Nanette's only marking is under her hair:

ARMAND MARSEILLE
Germany
390
A.   7½   M.

Nanette now belongs to Mrs. Stephen Salatich of Reseda, California.

Linda
Armand Marseille—24 Inch

LINDA is an early A & M. *Made in Germany* over a horseshoe mark and *Hd. 3 H.* are incised on back of her bisque shoulderplate. Her sawdust-filled kid body is unmarked but nice; rivet-jointed at hip and knee, lower legs and feet of muslin. Lower arms bisque—elbow gussets.

Her beautiful bisque face is nicely modeled and tinted; mouth open, tiny teeth, lovely brown sleeping eyes, real lashes. She greatly resembles a real child, Linda, who plays at our house, and both have naturally curly, shoulder-length brown hair. The doll has a ventilated wig—made like a transformation.

NANETTE AND LINDA

The old black fabrikoid doll buggy dates around 1900. A 1905 magazine photograph shows an identical white one.

Linda's soft yellow cotton dress and chartreuse silk bonnet are black
ribbon trimmed. Sheer white lace stockings show below her pantalettes
and black patent leather slippers cover her little fat feet.

Linda has joined the collection of Mrs. Helen Long of Van Nuys,
California. The old carriage now belongs to Mrs. Paul L. Wood of
Sepulveda, California.

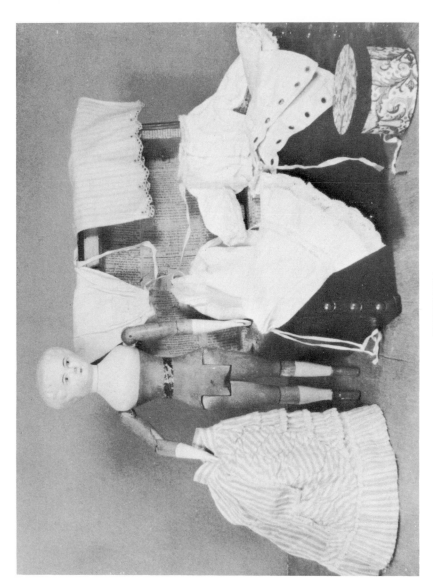

THERESA

Theresa
Mason and Taylor—11½ Inch

Theresa, who travels frequently, checks through her wardrobe and finds she's short of unmentionables. Obviously!

She always uses her great-aunt Mehitable's trunk, a real oldie. The lining is a Boston newspaper dated November 10, 1831. How's that for age?

Theresa does have a beautiful cotton skirt to wear on her trip. It is pink and white stripe with so many tucks, pleats and lace-edged ruffles that it stands alone! There are curved panel effects on each side and it should be worn with several full underskirts and perhaps a modest bustle. Note that it is longer in back. Most fashionable and up to the minute— an 1880 minute, that is! All Theresa's clothes are very old, well made and interesting but not original.

A Mason and Taylor she is, produced in the early 1880's in Springfield, Vt. Her body and limbs are of wood, fully and wonderfully jointed. The joints are a combination of ball and socket, mortice and tenon, with recesses and stops. Each hip joint is secured with a steel screw. She sits squarely, and her knees flex well. She can stand alone and is real fun to handle. Her arms will swing a full circle at the shoulders. Hands and feet are pewter, hands and part of lower arms painted flesh color. Legs painted flesh; feet, modeled like boots with heels, are painted bright blue. Her hands are rather straight, thumbs separate.

Theresa's shoulders, chest, neck and face are also flesh color. Eyes are blue with corner dots; mouth closed, nostrils tinted. Her molded golden hair is center-parted, brought in scallops down over the ears (if there were any) with short vertical curls all around the back.

Most of the Mason and Taylor heads had a wooden core covered with a thick composition coating in which the features were molded. This one is no exception. It swivels, too, clear around!

There are no markings left but around the waist is the characteristic black paper band which once bore the dates of all the patents.

Theresa and her accessories are from the collection of Mrs. Marianne De Nuñez of Arleta, California.

See: Eleanor St. George. *The Dolls of Yesterday*, Chapter 3.

MILDRED AND HELEN ELIZABETH

Mildred

Kling and Co. Blond Bisque—19 Inch

Mildred (left) and Helen Elizabeth made two little girls very happy long ago. They were purchased in 1897 in New Orleans by a young lady for her little sisters in Illinois. The present owner of both dolls is a daughter of one of those sisters. How nice to have two such lovelies from one's own family!

Mildred has the only mark. On back of her shoulderplate is a bell with the letter *K* inside. She was manufactured by Kling and Company of Ohrdruf, Thuringia. One concludes that she was made in the late 1880's, shipped into this country before 1891 and spent considerable time in storage or in store stock or both, until that exciting day in 1897.

Mildred's modeling and tinting are exquisite and the bisque is smooth. There are deep comb marks in her glazed, spun-taffy-colored, short hairdo. Mouth closed; stationary eyes brown and beautiful; nostrils and eye corners dotted. Her almost hidden ears have wee ruby earrings.

The white kid body has rivets at elbows and gussets at rump and knees; lower legs and feet of muslin; lower arms and hands of tinted, dimpled bisque.

Mildred's beautiful dress is an exact copy in old materials of an authentic child's dress of the 1880's. It is gray taffeta with two rows of three inch pleats for the skirt. The long-sleeved, long coat effect is also silk, a soft red and green plaid, edged with fine lace and tiny red French knots. There are five decorative plaid buttons down the center front and a large ruby velvet bow over the hips in back. Snow-white lacy tucked undies, white silk stockings and new hand-made white kid boots complete her outfit.

See: Luella Hart. *Directory of German Dolls*, p 3.

"Up in James' Room"

Helen Elizabeth
German Blond Bisque—20 Inch

Helen and Mildred, about the same age, have the same type bodies. Both have short molded hair, although Helen's is unglazed, has larger waves and deeper convolutions. Helen Elizabeth's turned shoulderhead, of paler bisque, has Parian-like texture. Set-in eyes are a very pretty dark blue, nostrils and eye corners dotted, mouth closed, chin dimpled.

Heln's authentic copy of a child's frock is similar in style to Mildred's, yet there are differences such as the dark blue satin front, shirred from neck to low waistline, and the large sailor collar of old ivory lace. There is a row of dark blue pearl buttons on either side of the shirring on the body of the coat-dress, which is of tiny gray check silk. Three rows of 1½ inch pleating form the skirt. There is a large blue satin soft knot across the rump; a self-bow of gray on the left side.

Helen's tucked undies are unbleached muslin with a real full petticoat and scads of luscious hand crocheted edging in ivory silk, 1½ inches wide! She has black silk stockings and new black kid tie shoes, handmade.

These children are from the collection of Mrs. Margaret Wright of Sherman Oaks, California.

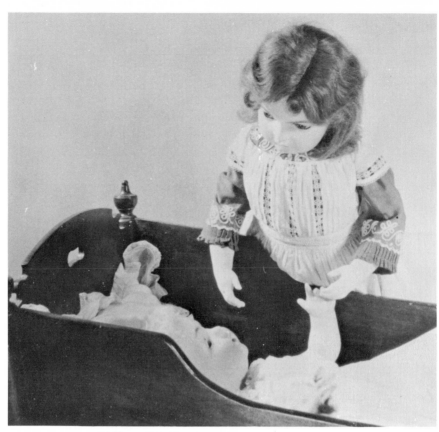

"Where Did You Come From, Baby Dear?"
LOUISE AND BABY THELMA

QUEUE SAN BABIES

Queue San Babies

Norimura Bros.—3⅓ to 4¾ Inch

THESE cunning all bisque babies were the answer of Norimura Bros. (N.Y.) to the "Kewpie" craze. They were registered on November 10, 1915, #90,565 and two of the babies still have paper labels on their fat tummies. The labels are red, diamond shape and say *QUEUE SAN BABY, Reg. U.S. Pat. Off.* I believe they were made in Germany for two reasons. In the first place the flesh colored bisque is good quality like that of the Kewpies. Then, I have seen two others, identical with the ones pictured, who have red triangular labels which read *CHIN CHIN—GERMANY.* These are probably earlier, before a trademark was registered here.

The interesting thing is that these obviously Chinese babies with black molded queues down most of their backs were originated by Japanese, made in Germany and registered in the U.S.! Cosmopolitan kiddies!

Queue San Babies have piquant little faces. The modeling and painting is excellent—even the eyelids are molded. Their eyes slant and eyebrows are unusually slanted, quite distinctive.

These babies have Kewpie-like arms, shoulder jointed, with outspread fingers, except the third and fourth. Their chubby legs have molded strapless slippers with pointed toes. They are painted pretty pastel colors and so are their molded bonnets. All painting is fired in the bisque.

The kneeling boy is barefoot, with cunning toes and a little round rear. The boy on the box is dressed and original. His mandarin-type gown is moss-green silk with a self-pattern of leaves. It is embroidered down the front and around the cuffs with shiny gold thread. Down the shoulder seams to the cuffs is a row of tiny black beads, simulating buttons. Very effective!

Make your own title for this picture. Is the mandarin blessing the children; is he leading them in song or just keeping the kneeling boy from opening the Japanese chest?

These oriental cherubs are from the collection of Mrs. Pat Schoonmaker of North Hollywood, California.

See: "U.S. Doll Trademarks, 1913–1950" by Luella Hart in *Spinning Wheel,* September, 1955.

"While Walking in the Park One Day—"   DAISY

Daisy
Unmarked German Bisque Fashion—20 Inch

D AISY'S unusually pale coloring, closed mouth, bisque dome, set-in brown eyes and lack of marking except #7 show she is very old. Also, as a friend remarked, "She looks very Simon and Halbigish!" and according to recent findings some of them were *really* old. Her shoulderhead is stationary; tinting very light but complete. There is a small hole on the top of her head where a wig could have been fastened. There are no sew holes on the shoulderplate. Her forearms and hands are bisque replacements.

Daisy's body is also old. Examination showed it once had a papier-mâché head. It seems to be machine sewn, at least partly, and is well made with a nipped-in waist—upper and lower legs sewn on by hand. The fine white cotton body is stuffed with vegetable fiber, perhaps moss.

Daisy's fairly new human hair wig is much more blond then it appears in the photograph and she is dressed in the style of the early 1900's. There is a reason for this. While I feel she is around 90 years old, I bought her to dress like a picture of my mother taken in 1902. The new white organdy dress is an exact copy of the one in Mom's picture, pigeon-breasted front, tiny waist, lace yolk and all. The full lacy jabot is flower trimmed. The upswept hairdo with four little curls on top is like my mother's and there is a parasol in the old picture also. Daisy's undies have lace, tucks and embroidery AND she wears a white satin corset! She has real white silk stockings and handmade white kid slippers; scalloped around the top, rosetted and lined with pink silk. Her dress and slips are much longer in back than in front—a small train!

The *real* Daisy used to say, "I led the grand ball in this dress."

See: "Simon & Halbig, Master Craftsmen" by Genevieve Angione in *Spinning Wheel* beginning December, 1962.

LITA AND NITA

Lita and Nita

J. D. Kestner Twins—24 Inch

T<small>HIS</small> picture should be in color. The background is powder blue, old wicker chair pale pink and twins' dresses, lilac. Add the delicate tinting of faces and hands, the ecru lace yokes and golden mohair wigs—luscious!

They are all original and alike except for color of sleep-eyes, and that blue-eyed Nita (right) lost her lavender hairbows. Lita's eyes are brown.

These fine turned shoulderheads have smooth bisque, softly tinted; open mouths, nostril and eye dots, four teeth, chin dimples. Faces are broad with considerable fullness under the chins. Plaster domes have never been disturbed. Under the wig is incised the letter *K*. There are two holes for tying eyes in shipping on back of the head. On bottom of the shoulderplate in back, well hidden by an inch of kid is *Made in Germany* and a large *K*.

The twins' bodies are the finest heavy white kid, still soft and pliable, filled with ground cork. Hands and arms are bisque, well modeled, dimpled and dainty. Size 7 is incised on the rounded inner side of each elbow. The shoulder structure is interesting. There is a round hardwood shaft (with a socket at each end) laid across the top of the body. Upper arms of hardwood, kid covered, have a stationary ball to fit the shaft socket. Heavy rubber runs from one arm through the shaft and down into the other arm. The shaft is held in place by an inner cotton body casing or sack. The bisque shoulderhead fits down over the wooden shaft onto the cloth-covered cork-filled body and is fastened at the two sew holes, back and front. The outside kid body covering comes up over the whole, the bisque shoulder held securely in place by inch-wide tabs of kid which cross on top and are sewn tightly.

Their beautiful long wool dresses are very full. Two rows of lavender ribbon decorate the skirts; narrow sleeves have lace puffs, elbow to wrist. The underclothes are rich with trimming—white rickrack and lace on chemises, wide hand crocheted lace on panties and underskirts.

They have no shoes. Perhaps they never did. Their chubby cotton feet and legs are encased in long stockings—Lita, old black cotton lace, Nita, blue wool hand knits, replacements, I suspect. Lost her hairbows too, remember?

The twins and chair are from the collection of Mrs. Roy Cowdrey Sr. of Panorama City, California.

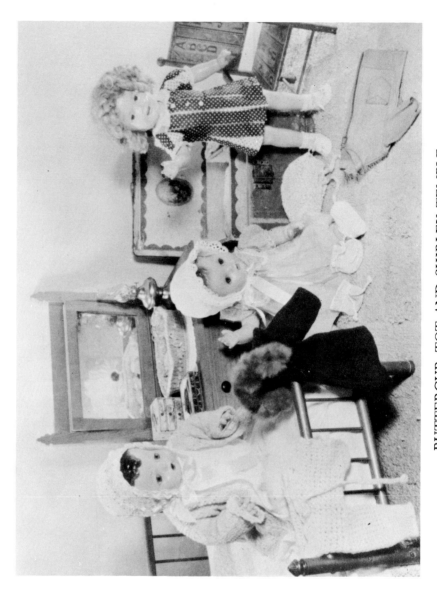

BUTTERCUP, TOT AND SHIRLEY TEMPLE

Buttercup
Horsman Baby—13½ Inch (seated)

Buttercup, on the bed, is one of three dolls in this picture bought for my daughter as a small child. The trademark "Buttercup" was registered on April 17, 1926, #230,327 by George Borgfeldt Co., of New York. The mark *H © C* embossed on back of her neck is a clue to her maker, Horsman. Some heads were marked *E. I. H. Co.* The head (with flange neck), curved arms and legs are composition; the body of unbleached muslin tightly stuffed with kapok.

Buttercup is a distinctive looking doll—at least that's why I bought her in 1932. Her large nearly round eyes were blue but over the years have turned kelly green. They have hair lashes and sleep. Her little round knob of a nose is babyish and her open mouth shows a molded tongue. She never had teeth. Molded hair is painted a soft brown; nostrils and eye corners are tinted. Her arms and legs have little chubby creases; fat fingers are partially separated, all fingers and toes dimpled. Jointed at hips and shoulders, she sits quite solidly.

Buttercup wears my daughter's baby dress and *her* son's pale green sacque and booties. This dolly has the original clothes she came in, however, and two or three other dresses of the same period, plus many hand crotcheted items: jackets, caps, and booties. These have always been kept in the little old trunk. It originally belonged to my great-aunt who gave it to me when I was ten. In turn, it became my daughter's and is now temporarily in my collection. That 98-year-old doll trunk could tell family history! It has a rounded top, a divided tray and its original key.

The brass doll bed is dated 1892, on all four posts. The doll dresser is older and has a handblown mirror. The white bedspread is oldest of all, hand loomed in the South before the Civil War.

I forgot to mention Buttercup's real baby cap—courtesy Goodwill Industries. It is hand crocheted of ivory silk with white ribbons woven through the beading—a soft, crushable little cap that feels good in your hand.

Buttercup, Tot and Shirley have always belonged to Mrs. K. M. Murray, Jr., of Newhall, California.

Tot

American Composition Toddler—20 Inch

Tot, purchased at Christmas time in 1937, is all composition, beautifully designed, perfectly proportioned. A sturdy toddler, she stands alone easily. All extremities have fat wrinkles and dimples; knees are still rosy tinted. She is jointed at neck, shoulders and hips. Her clothes are new—blue nylon dress, blue short socks and white slippers. She has a white piqué bonnet with lace and embroidery trim. Her original pink and blue piqué dress is in the old trunk:

Tot's face is friendly and smiling. Her pretty open mouth shows two teeth and a red felt tongue. Sleeping blue eyes have long hair lashes; dark shading above. Her wee nose turns slightly upward; molded hair is tinted a soft brown. Her head came from the same mold as a talking doll I once owned, but it was unmarked, too. Who made her?

Shirley Temple

Ideal Portrait Doll—19½ Inch

Shirley's gray sleeping eyes, in good condition, have long hair lashes. Her silky mohair wig (the earlier pale blond type) is also in good shape. She is jointed at shoulder, hip and neck. Both arms curve, the right more than the left. Her hands are dimpled, thumbs separate; entire doll, composition. The mouth is open, smiling, showing six teeth; dimples at either side. Nostrils are dotted; a red line appears above each eyelid.

Shirley was designed by Bernard Lipfert, and first copyrighted on October 24, 1934, #357,464 by the Ideal Novelty and Toy Co. of Brooklyn, New York. This one was purchased December, 1935.

She has quite a wardrobe, made about that time—a short leather coat, a dark red wool coat (silk-lined with a fur collar) and many crocheted garments. In the picture Shirley wears a blue and white polka dot cotton print which hangs pleated from the shoulder with puffed sleeves and a white organdy collar, lace-edged. There are three tiny buttons down the front. Her white shoes and socks are new.

See: "The Original Shirley Temple Doll" by Pat Schoonmaker in the *Doll Guild Review*, February and June, 1961.

CLOTILDE

Clotilde

Wax over composition—17 Inch

I s this the "Queen of the May" complete with diadem? Well, no, just a demure little wax doll who loves flowers. What looks like a crown on her soft brown mohair is simply a rosette of pale blue satin ribbon. Her turned shoulderhead is wax-coated composition with no opening on top and no marking. Her intense blue eyes are glass and sleep. Their color is very like ball bluing my mother used. She has a closed mouth, rosy cheeks and a full double chin.

Clotilde has a muslin body, straw stuffed. There is an oblong wooden squeaker to press on her tummy—to no avail. Arms and legs from elbow and knee down are composition. The upper part is like the body. She is jointed only at hip and shoulders.

Clotilde's original dainty white dress has had the torn lace replaced with a flounce of beautiful old embroidery. A Mother Hubbard type frock with a narrow belt of insertion and a very full skirt, are perfect for her era—between 1870 and 1880. A wide self-sash ties in back with unusually long streamers. The sleeves are three-quarter length.

Clotilde belongs to Mrs. Ellery C. Thorpe of Glendale, California.

See: Eleanor St. George. *Old Dolls*, Chapter VI.
    Jo Elizabeth Gerken. *Wonderful Dolls of Wax*, p. 10.

"Tea Time"   BABETTE, JANET AND TONI

Babette
Simon & Halbig—K (Star) R—17 Inch

Babette is really big enough to serve at a tea party, as you can see. In the picture with her dolls, she looks like a toddler. Her dollies are tiny old German all-bisques, mostly unmarked. In her right hand is a modern German celluloid.

Babette is a late doll, with a short thigh piece and a joint *above* the knee. Otherwise, her fully ball-jointed excellent composition body is like the ones *before* World War I. She is marked *Simon & Halbig— K (Star) R—Germany* on back of her head and *403–43* at the base of her neck.

Two points of interest: her nice little hands are rubber and her blue eyes, different. The iris and pupil are embedded much deeper than in the average German eye, giving her a soulful expression, to be a bit trite! However, it's true that they are unusual and beautiful. She has real lashes and sleeps.

Babette's quality bisque is quite pale and delicately tinted. She has fine modeling, open mouth, four teeth, nostril dots, black painted lashes and brown eyebrows—a pretty child.

All little girls should have soft, wavy, golden hair like Babette's. This mohair wig, I believe, is original.

She wears a pale blue dotted Swiss dress, very full, lace trimmed, with short puffed sleeves. The white organdy pinafore has a lace bib. Her black tie shoes are patent leather; her socks white rayon.

Wasn't it fortunate that the camera was handy when the butterfly flew in the open window?

BABETTE

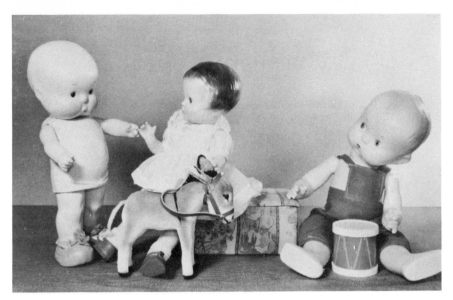

"Eternal Triangle"   HEbee-SHEbee, PATSY JR. AND SKIPPY

HEbee-SHEbee
Horsman—10½ Inch

T<small>HE</small> eternal triangle, that's what we have here. Before the appearance of the kid with the blue booties, Patsy was duly impressed by Skippy's prowess with the drum. Skippy's jealousy has colored his thinking to the point where he can't see that it isn't the ball-headed, scantily-clad kid that enchants Patsy, but the kid's cunning gray donkey. Ah me! That's life.

C. H. Twelvetrees designed this boy. Check the "Twelvetrees Kiddies" in old *Pictorial Reviews*. He is smooth composition (booties and shirt, too), elastic cord jointed at neck, shoulders and hips. Bootie ties are blue yarn. Cheeks, nose, knees and fingers are rosy tinted. His painted blue eyes with large black vertical oval pupils, and tiny mouth give him a sober appearance.

HEbee-SHEbee was patented by E. I. Horsman, Inc., New York, in 1925, #223,918. He has no marking but is pictured in Horsman's 1960 brochure "Dolls Your Grandmother Loved."

I'm counting on the little velvet donkey to smooth things over!

See: "E. I. Horsman, Father of the Doll Industry" by Elizabeth A. Coleman in *Antiques Journal* for January, 1963.
"HEbee SHEbees—Real American Kids" by Gladys Hollander in *Antiques Journal* for August, 1964.

Patsy Jr.
EFFanBEE—11½ Inch

THE Patsy dolls were patented on October 14, 1927, by Fleischaker and Baum (EFFanBEE), New York, #256,080. They were designed by Herr Bernard Lipfert, a German who arrived in the United States in 1912, just when he was needed most. The new doll and toy industry was growing rapidly to overtake the German imports.

Over the years Herr Lipfert designed dozens and dozens of dolls (perhaps hundreds) for various dollmakers. He also designed almost as many *imitations* of his originals for those who wanted to make cheaper dolls. This explains a lot of similar-looking dolls which have puzzled the collector from time to time.

Patsy dolls were made in many sizes and several varieties. This one is Patsy Jr. She is of nice quality composition, jointed at head, shoulders and hips. Both arms are curved—the right much more than the left. Her painted hair is brown—molded in a shingle-bob with bangs. Painted eyes (round and blue), tiny mouth, pink cheeks. Embossed on her shoulder is *EFFanBEE PATSY JR. DOLL.*

Patsy's cotton clothes are new. The dainty apron is white organdy, lace trimmed; dress is pale lemon cotton with a self-stripe. She has darling brown leather sandals and white socks.

Patsy Jr. is now in the collection of Mrs. Kay Sigrud of Granada Hills, California.

See: "The Patsy Doll" by Pat Schoonmaker in the *Doll Guild Review*, August, 1960.
  "Dolls—Made in America" in *Fortune*, December, 1936.

Skippy
EFFanBEE—13½ Inch

SKIPPY was a well known and loved comic strip character by P. L. Crosby. On his shoulders is embossed *EFFanBEE PATSY Pat. Pen. Doll.* The back of the head reads *EFFanBEE SKIPPY, circle C, P. L. Crosby.*

"Skip" is composition, jointed at hips, shoulders and neck; arms curved. His painted blue eyes, wide open, look sharply to the right.

Peaked eyebrows give him a quizzical look. His molded hair is golden with one long lock extending down his forehead to a point between his eyebrows.

Skippy's a cute child in his turkey red overalls. "Universal Boy with Bare Feet," you might say.

He now belongs to Mrs. Marianne De Nuñez of Arleta, California.

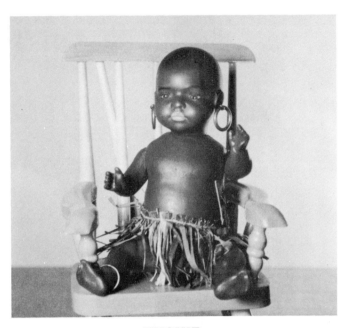

HUGHIE

Hughie
Heubach Köppelsdorf Colored Baby—5¾ Inch (seated)

Hughie is a changling. This is his original outfit: a varicolored raffia skirt (nailed in back), his brass anklet and earrings. At home, however, he wears a long pink baby dress and a crocheted pink wool sacque with matching cap. This goes on over his original outfit. The earrings tuck under his cap and then he looks like any cute Negro baby.

This cunning child has an extremely well shaped dark brown bisque head, Negroid features and fat little cheeks. He has painted black hair, lashes and brows; brown sleep-eyes with black pupils; tiniest red nostril and eye corner dots; a closed mouth with bright red lips.

Hughie's composition semi-curved-leg baby body is brown, the same shade as his head. He is jointed at shoulders and hips and the modeling is quite good. Especially nice are his hands and feet.

Incised on back of his head is: *Heubach Koppelsdorf—399–16/0 Germany, D.R.G.M.*

His date is probably in the late 1920's. Montgomery Ward sold a doll for 69¢ which looks identical (Catalog 115, Fall and Winter, 1931–1932) calling it a wild baby from the South Seas—a cannibal child—ugh! *My* dear little Hughie?

JANET AND LINDA BABY

Janet

Simon & Halbig—K (Star) R—Flirty Eye—20 Inch

Janet's gorgeous brown eyes are one of her nicest features, along with her fluffy blond human hair wig. It is fine textured, naturally curly and fits around her head in soft waves; original, I think.

This motherly child holds "Linda Baby," a modern Terri Lee Doll (6½ inch, seated). In the tea party picture, where Toni took the spoons, you can see Janet's two-piece middy suit better. It is of dark blue wool serge, bloused at the waist, with a large sailor collar, high neck and a dickey in front. The suit is trimmed in all the right places with red silk braid, stars, bars and anchors (hand done) and has a row of tiny brass buttons down the front of the blouse. Practically all the machine stitching is done in white, purposely, pocket and all. Very effective! Did you have a middy suit like this? I did—and didn't it itch? Remember?

Janet's face is smooth flesh-colored bisque, very well modeled. Her cheeks are rosy, chin dimpled, nostrils and eye corners tinted, mouth open, red tongue and four little teeth. Eyebrows are soft brown, lashes painted black. Her eyes look from side to side and she sleeps, too, but the lids are a separate mechanism. I'm sure they once had real lashes. On back of her head are two holes, for tying the eyes in shipping. Also on the back of her head is the incising: *SIMON & HALBIG—K (six pointed star) R.* The absence of the word *Germany* could date her before 1891. The number 53 appears at the base of her neck.

This doll's fully ball-jointed composition body is well proportioned and in very nice condition. On her feet are black silk socks and old black leather slippers.

Janet is now in the collection of Mrs. Phyllis Roberts of Reseda, California.

See: "K & R German Doll Manufacturers" in *Doll Talk*, January and February, 1962.
   "History of K & R" in *Doll Talk*, March–April, 1962.
   "The Kämmer and Reinhardt Dolls" by Pat Schoonmaker in *Doll News*, beginning February, 1965.

Claudette
All Bisque French Fashion—5 Inch

THESE pictures were taken in Claudette's dressing room at the theater. She keeps her birdcage there and has the poodles with her at all performances. Froufrou, who chewed Claudette's kid boot, is in disgrace. Consequently, only Fifi walks in the park today.

Claudette has a bisque socket-head, long slender arms and legs jointed at shoulders and hips; a cork cap and set-in bright blue eyes. Her face, too, is slender and her neck, long. She is definitely a lady doll, probably a doll-house doll of the Eighties or Nineties. She is well modeled with smooth bisque, delicate tinting, rosy cheeks, closed mouth, and the tiniest nostril and inner eye corner dots. Fingers and toes are defined. Her

CLAUDETTE AND FIFI

CLAUDETTE AND FROUFROU

golden hair is long, but she wears it upswept with a chignon in back; a replacement wig of fine human hair. Her old blond wig, still around, looks like last year's bird nest!

Claudette is devastating in her long sweeping pegnoir of gray and white striped taffeta! It is old, trimmed with narrow ivory lace, magenta silk binding and bands of black velvet ribbon $\frac{1}{16}$ of an inch wide—that's right, $\frac{1}{16}$ of an inch! Oh yes, there's a bow of magenta ribbon at the breast, and a larger one with streamers on her rump. Quite a gown!

Her little three-piece outfit is new, of white cotton net, lace trimmed. The matching hat has a pink bow; small shoes are white kid.

Claudette has size *0* incised on back of her head and again in the middle of her back. The numbers may be *nothing* but this little lady is *something!*

MONA LISA

Mona Lisa
Colored Jolly Doll—20 Inch

Mona Lisa is the namesake of a real little colored girl, old enough to be a bride herself by now.

I found *this* Mona Lisa in a toy store in an outlying district. She attracted my attention first because her clothes were so lovely, next because she herself was so dainty and well designed. She has no Negroid features but her soft color is appropriate, her brown sleeping eyes with black lashes are good and her little black saran cap of short imbedded curls is just perfect. Ears are pierced and have pendant pearl eardrops. There are deep nostril indentations and her pretty mouth is well modeled and closed.

Mona is jointed at neck, shoulders and hips. Her long legs are shapely and slender and her feet are formed to fit her high-heeled white plastic toeless sandals. Toes with nails are well designed and her hands with fingers apart are also nicely done. She can clasp her bridal bouquet with both hands, fingers entwined. Vinyl plastic makes this possible, of course.

Her bridal dress is white rayon satin, floor length. Bodice is also satin with a yoke of flower-patterned net. The same net makes lacy panels clear to the floor on either side of her skirt. Silver threads are interwoven with white flowers and narrow dainty silver and white satin braid outlines the panel and yoke edges. White satin ribbons hang to the floor from her bouquet. Mona Lisa's dainty nylon net veil is waist length and falls from a white satin, braid-trimmed circle cap. It is tied on her black ringlets by white satin ribbon with a bow in back.

Doesn't she sound like a quality doll? Well she is—and adorable to boot! Mona Lisa was for sale in 1958 but may have appeared before that date. She was made by Jolly Toys Inc. of New York, N.Y.

Mona Lisa lives in the crowded bedroom of Janet and Gail Corwin of Arleta, California.

JULIE LORINE AND GOLDIE

Julie Lorine

Celluloid Kämmer and Reinhardt—12½ Inch

Julie, let that doll's shoe alone! What have you done with your *own* shoes and socks?"

That Julie—she's a shoe and sock remover! They're hard to live with, I can tell you! Of course, it's my fault. She's adorable and it's hard to punish her—so what can one expect?

This is the cutest celluloid doll. Embossed on her head, in back, is the six pointed star with K on one side and R on the other—also 735/33 and *Germany*. K (*Star*) R and 33 is embossed between her shoulder blades, also.

Julie's flesh-colored body and head are beautifully molded of heavy celluloid. There are dimples, fat creases and chubbiness in all the right places on this straight-legged toddler. Her dark blond bobbed hair with bangs is mohair and original. The Dutch bob is perhaps the only clue, except *Germany*, to her age. She probably dates somewhere within the second decade of this century.

There are blue sleep-eyes, real lashes, rosy cheeks, eye and nostril dots, tiny open mouth in a pronounced cupid's bow, and two teeth on this fat-cheeked socket-head. She is jointed with elastic at neck, shoulders and hips. Her arms are the regular curved baby type; life-like legs, feet and toes.

Julie's all-lace petticoat and sleeveless knit undershirt are very "little girl" looking.

Goldie, the 5½ inch all-bisque golden haired dolly is an old German one, although unmarked. She has bright blue set eyes, closed mouth, rosy cheeks, blue molded slippers and pink socks. The bisque is pale and smooth; hips and shoulders jointed. Her coral corduroy dress has a pleated silk skirt and tiny pearl buttons.

Both dolls and accessories are from the collection of Mrs. Robert Burckert of Sylmar, California.

COLETTE AND EMILE

Colette

S.F.B.J. Toddler—28 Inch

THESE life-size toddlers are charming. Colette, especially, is so cuddly, partly due to the lovely unmarked composition body, fully jointed and chubby. The forearm is wood, lathe turned, well designed, with attached wooden ball. The toes are well defined, dimpled—the big one turns 'way up. Her wrists are jointed, separate fingers well shaped and dimpled. Her thighs have a wide diagonal hip joint. This, combined with the sturdy lower leg with attached ball at knee joint, gives her maximum movability.

Colette's bisque head has a soft sheen. Open-closed mouth has two molded upper teeth and a small smile. Blue sleep-eyes have long lashes; cheeks pink; nostril and eye corner dots. The eyebrows are a departure from 19th century ones: shorter, narrower and lighter, more natural.

Her beautiful human hair (cork cap) is golden and curls up all the way around. Incising on back of her neck:

FRANCE
S.F.B.J.
24
PARIS

Her date is probably after World War I because of late thigh pieces.

Colette's new pink calico dress has a short yoke, lace-edged puffed sleeves and full-gathered skirt. There is a matching bonnet. Her dainty white embroidered pinafore is old; socks white, slippers pink silk.

"Christening Party"

Emile

S.F.B.J. Pouty Toddler—27½ Inch

Part of Emile's appeal is his slightly bewildered look. He hasn't learned to share. Knows about grabbing, however!

Emile's bisque head is very like that of Colette's but his pouty mouth is closed, set-in eyes lighter blue. On back of his head is incised:

21
S.F.B.J.
252
PARIS
12

In blue ink on his back:

JUMEAU
MÉDAILLE D'OR
PARIS

Emile's body is old, perhaps brought to the S.F.B.J. combine in 1899. It is papier-mâché, with stiff wrists, large thick hands and fingers—jointed at shoulders, hips, knees and elbows. He has a toddler body, chubby, sturdy, but shy on flexibility.

His blue and white suit with short blue button-on pants dates, like the head, roughly around World War I. The trademark S.F.B.J. #91052 was registered July 17, 1905, but was used from 1899.

Emile has platinum blond mohair (cork cap) finger-length curls, wavy bangs. His handmade shoes are high bronze kid with three straps, milk glass buttons, silver buckles, leather soles.

Colette, Emile and toys belong to Mrs. Thelma Bouchey of Toluca Lake, California.

GLORIA AND ABBY

Gloria
Ravon Walking Doll (Modern)—19 Inch

GLORIA is a beautiful doll made of hard, unbreakable butyrate plastic, finely designed, proportioned and modeled. Her legs swing freely at the hips, and she walks easily when the weight is shifted from one foot to the other. She can sit, stand alone and do the splits. A spiral spring arrangement permits this movement which involves only the legs. The neck and shoulders are jointed also.

Her hands and arms are darling—fingers separate and realistic, showing nails, lines, joints, with dimples at the base. Palms and wrists are fully delineated. Her brown sleep-eyes and lashes are plastic, have dark shading above, giving a soft expression. Her open mouth shows a red felt tongue and four teeth. Knees, cheeks and backs of hands are tinted.

"And her golden hair was hanging down her back." That's true. It's also true that it is modern Dynel, but original, suitable and attractive. The hair came in several colors on these dolls; eyes brown or blue, and there was a colored doll, same model.

Gloria's handmade red and white print dress has a pocket lined with red organdy and a bow of the same at her throat. Her socks are red; slippers black, with buckles and bows.

Gloria, unmarked, was patented (#589139) October 31, 1950, as "Little Miss Gadabout" and made by Artisan Novelty Co. of Gardena, California, until 1956. Their 1951 catalog has eleven illustrations of Ravon Walking Dolls dressed in lovely clothing. The Bride retailed at $26.95, while the undressed doll sold for $15.95. There were thirteen costumes labeled *California Originals* by Michele, selling from $3.95 to $10.95. Mr. Howard Black was the designer and creator of these "Raving Beauty Dolls." Three names for one doll!

Abby, the lightweight celluloid curved-leg baby, has *Made in USA* embossed on her back, probably a Japanese mark. She is chubby and dimpled with dear little hands and feet. Her original Dutch bob is brown mohair. She has painted blue eyes, rosy cheeks; mouth closed; 7 inches (seated).

Abby now belongs to Mrs. Paul L. Wood of Sepulveda, California.

See: "Today's Doll Market" in *Doll Guild Review* for March and April, 1955.
"Story of a Modern Doll Factory" by Mary D. Berry in *Doll Guild Review*, January and February, 1960.
"U.S. Doll Trade Marks, 1913–1950" by Luella Hart in *Spinning Wheel* for May, 1956.
Luella Hart. *Directory of British Dolls*, p. 49.
"Celluloid Dolls and Doll Heads" by Luella Hart in *Toy Trader* for May, 1954.

Chérie

Limoges French Bisque—13½ Inch

For a change, here is a description of Chérie from my information sheet just as I jotted it down:

Fully ball-jointed composition body
Bisque head, cork cap, pierced ears
Open mouth with four teeth—nostril dots
Very large, medium-blue eyes, blown glass, stationary
Blond mohair wig—original
Hands—dainty, with long fingers
Pink cotton socks—white leather slippers
Hat—straw—multicolored ribbon
White dress—lace and embroidery—pink sash, side tie

Well, that's all true, but you should hold this little French child in your hands. She is darling; the word "dainty" was coined for her. See the graceful hands and slender fingers. Her white lacy skirt, with pink organdy flounce, is trimmed *underneath* with two rows of narrow pink ribbon; different and very Frenchy. The color peeks out through the lace now and then. The dainty waist is scalloped and embroidered at neck, sleeves and just below the sash. Her little hat has a rippled brim. *Très chic, n'est-ce pas?* Her over-size eyes have such an alive expression, she reminds me of Gisèle. They'd be a pair, those two!

High on the back of her head, incised in a box, is *FABRICATION FRANCAISE*. Below that, appears *AL&Cie*, under that, *LIMOGES*. Still lower is *CHÉRIE 3*. No doubt about her name! She was made in Limoges, France, by A. Lanternier and Co., probably between 1891 and 1914.

Chérie is enchanted with the tiny unmarked baby in the wicker cradle. He is German bisque, jointed at hips and shoulders, with open-closed mouth and painted blue eyes.

Both dolls and the lovely old cradle belong to Mrs. Ruby Sligh of Glendale, California.

See: Luella Hart. *Complete French Doll Dictionary*, p. 63.

CHÉRIE

PEACEFUL AND ABBY

Peaceful
Pre-Greiner—28 Inch

Iɴ the early 1840's, when an artist came to do her portrait, Peaceful was ready. She had arranged a few prized possessions on the table to be included in the painting; wore her gold locket—and black silk mitts! Abby, her baby (described elsewhere) did a bit of squirming before the sitting was finished.

Peaceful used to sit in a chair by my bed. Every time I entered the room, her serene face gave me a feeling of peace—hence, her name. The calm expression comes partly from her dark brown eyes (blown glass, pupilless) and partly from the soft sweep of her black molded hair. It is parted in the center and brought around behind her ears, falling in soft vertical curls around the back.

Peaceful has the nicest body I've seen on a primitive; entirely hand-made and beautifully designed. The wide shoulders slope down to a small waist. The separately-made wide rump has three vertical seams in back and one down the front. Consequently, she sits well. Her knees and hips are stitch-jointed, feet are made with seams at the instep and around the sole. Toes, too, are stitch-indicated. Someone spent hours on the meticulously overcast seams. Her arms and hands are white kid, all ten fingers separate.

The same skilled needle-woman must have made her clothing. The pale pink print dress is covered with wee rose polka dots and down the front are thirteen tiny three-hole buttons, rose and white. The top under-skirt is scalloped eyelet embroidery with dozens of six-petaled flowers, cut out, and buttonholed by hand. Such industry! The old black leather baby slippers are the kind with no indication of left or right. The toes have scalloped leather bows.

This all original, quaint old papier-mâché (with the calming influence) is now in the collection of Mrs. Muriel Rahmn, of Sherman Oaks, California.

See: Eleanor St. George. *Dolls of Three Centuries*, p. 142.

JESSIE AND JACKIE TAR

Jackie Tar
All Bisque—5½ Inch

Jackie's a handsome boy—flowing gold ringlets—wavy bangs, blue eyes and rosy cheeks. He came from a fine mold but whoever finished him must have been in a hurry. More time and care spent in sanding and tinting and he would have been an exquisite little figure.

Nevertheless, he is still cute in his white, long-sleeve, bloused sailor suit with short pants and cap, molded and sky-blue trimmed. His high boots are blue with ribbed socks peeking over the top. Fingers and thumbs well defined but not separated; wire jointed at hips and shoulders. 40 1/1 is incised on the hip flange. The mouth is closed, nostrils tinted. Black eyelid lines, brown brows and deep chin dimple add to his charm.

The style of Jackie's clothes, hair and boots, and lack of further marking, all indicate his age before 1891.

These chunky children are from the collection of Mrs. Pat Schoonmaker of North Hollywood, California.

Jessie

All Bisque—6 Inch

J ESSIE is quite a stolid little girl—round-faced and German-looking. She is wire-jointed at hips and shoulders. Her only mark is #3 inside the hip flange but she looks 1920'ish. Perhaps a label disappeared.

Her bisque is very pale and of fair quality. Modeling and tinting are quite nice, especially her fluffy side-parted blond molded hair and blue hair bows. Eyes are painted blue, brows brown, mouth closed. Cheeks, nostrils and eye corners are tinted. Jessie's fingers are defined but unseparated. She has dimpled knees, molded brown strap slippers and white ribbed socks with blue garter line.

Jessie is dressed in yellow organdy for her picture with Jack. They had a tiff over the gold chair, however, and neither child smiled for the camera!

Biddy Pert

Peg Wooden—4¼ Inch

B IDDY Pert is a dear little lady doll from the Grodner Tal. She is tall and slender, jointed at knees, hips, shoulders and wrists but not at elbows. She has bright pink cheeks—after all those years!—and her quaint clothes are tacked on with tiny nails now rusted with age. Much of her ivory enamel is still intact. Her clothes, all precious old cotton prints, are gray with age and her white mob cap is adorable. It was tacked on, too, but it just had to come off to find out if there was a tuck comb. There was!

There are four different old prints in her costume. The skirt is a large pink and white floral, her shawl is a tiny blue and white floral. Her long sleeves are an even tinier pink and white floral and the tiniest of all is her large apron of white background covered with dozens of wee brown N's. There is a quarter-inch band of blue grosgrain tape around the bottom of her skirt.

Biddy was imported from England not long ago. She came in duty free and is the type of doll dressed by Queen Victoria. Her age? Well, the tag that came with her (from a reliable importer) says: "Tuck Comb Biddy Pert, all original, 1800" and this is believable.

See: Max von Boehn. *Dolls and Puppets*, rev. edn., Fig. 120.
   "Decline and Fall of Wooden Dolls" by Ruth E. and R. C. Mathes in *Doll Collector's Manual*, 1964, p. 24.

Millie

Milliner's Model—12½ Inch

THESE rigid primitive so-called "Milliner's Models," have a very definite charm all their own. It is interesting that there are so many of them and that they are so alike, differing almost entirely in hairdo and size alone.

Millie has the familiar wooden lower arms and legs and stiff white kid body, sawdust stuffed. Thumbs are the only digits separated—fingers just slightly defined. There is also the familiar colored band of tape which covers the joining of limbs to body—in this case, deep blue.

Her papier-mâché shoulderhead is enameled an ivory shade with painted features. She still has rosy cheeks and blue eyes, black eyebrows, closed mouth and a definite little chin. Her black molded hairdo is center-parted, drawn back to the front of her ears just below the eyeline. Long vertical curls go around from cheek to cheek, cover the ears and rest on her shoulders. She is really an attractive little doll, as they all are if you study them with an open mind and let their sweetness come through.

Millie's tan striped cotton voile dress, simply but fully gathered at neck and waist, may be original. Certainly it is very old. Her white cotton underskirt and lace trimmed pantalettes are old and everything is handmade. A bit of old narrow brown velvet ribbon forms her belt and ties in a bow in back. There are two one-inch-wide tucks around the bottom of her skirt.

The only movement these dolls were designed to have was a slight flexibility at the shoulders. Certainly they have no moveable joints in the real sense of the word and never could they have sat down.

According to recent findings, papier-mâché was first used for shoulderheads in Germany in 1807. The stiff kid bodies like Millie's were first made for these heads in 1820.

Millie, who dates around 1830 or so, likes to hob-nob with Biddy Pert—they have era and simplicity in common, among other things.

The old rocker looks handmade, has a woven rush seat and is stained a faded rust color.

See: "Early Papier Mâché" by Clara Hallard Fawcett in *Hobbies* for February, 1964.
  Doll Collectors Manual, 1956–1957, p. 61.

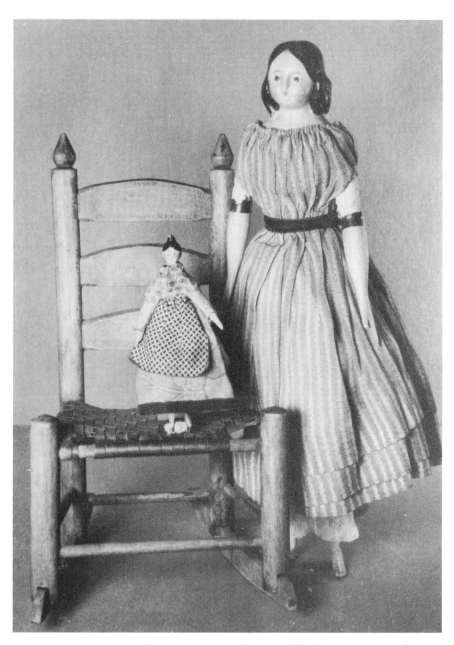

BIDDY PERT AND MILLIE

BABY THELMA

Baby Thelma
Simon and Halbig—K(Star)R—18 Inch (seated)

BABY Thelma has now retired. She was a model for many, many years in the baby section of a large department store in Los Angeles (first opened in 1883) and is still only one year old—size, that is.

She is a beautiful child with fine bisque, very large sleeping gray-blue eyes and original blond caracul wig. Her pretty open mouth shows two upper teeth and a bisque tongue. She has rosy cheeks with faint dimples; a larger one in her chin. Incised in large letters on back of her head is *K (Star) R—Simon & Halbig* and down on the neck, *121—62.*

Baby Thelma has the regulation curved-leg-and-arm composition body, with dimples in elbows, knees and feet. Toes are well modeled, big ones up-turned. Inside her body is a voice box, now quiet.

Thelma wears authentic old baby clothes, down to her long silk and wool stockings and adorable kid booties. Her lovely long dress is hand-made with row after row of lace and embroidery in alternate horizontal strips down the front panel. Between each strip is featherstitching—yards of it. There is a three inch flounce of rich heavy lace on the shawl collar of her wool coat. Notice that the lacy ruffles are longer and fuller at the top of her embroidered bonnet, dating it around 1900.

We could date Baby Thelma before 1891, there being no *Germany,* but she might have been picked up in Germany by someone a few years later. Who knows?

Bitsy
All Bisque—5 Inch

BITSY'S the one with long dark brown hair. She has curly bangs and a pink hair ribbon. It matches her pink lace dress.

She is just like Tiny except for having dark brown sleep-eyes and different markings. Her head is incised *150—4½0* and *150* is also inside her leg flange.

"It's a good thing that pony is gentle, Bitsy—you're standing directly behind him!"

Bitsy now belongs to Miss Arax Arklin of Granada Hills, California.

Tiny

All Bisque—4¾ Inch

A new pony! Is there a greater thrill in childhood? I doubt it, although it could be I feel that way being so equine-minded myself. Anyway, it's Tiny's turn to ride the pony and she's real brave for a little girl.

Tiny is jointed at shoulders and hips. Her arms are curved. Her bisque tinting and modeling are quite good; mouth closed, eyes painted blue. Inner eye corners and nostrils are dotted, tiny as she is. She has molded black slippers with heels and white high ribbed socks with a blue garter line at the top. Her mohair wig is medium-blond with bangs and quite long. Tiny's hat and dress are all white lace, pink ribbon trimmed.

On the back of her head is the marking: 257—11—SWC. This would date her before 1891, unless, of course, she once had a German label which came unglued. You decide!

Tiny has joined the collection of Mrs. Paul L. Wood of Sepulveda, California.

"New Pony"　　BITSY, TESSA, TINY, SWEETIE AND ELEANOR-ROSE

Tessa

All Bisque—7 Inch

Tessa is wearing her new pink organdy with a very deep hem, embroidered top, and lace around the neck and armholes. She has a matching bonnet but she dropped it somewhere in her excitement over the pony. You see, it's really hers—a birthday present. She rode him all morning before the children arrived for the party. Bet she'll be stiff tomorrow!

Tessa has a light brown mohair wig cut in a Dutch bob—no trouble and very becoming. She has nice bisque, good modeling, sleeping brown eyes, and an open mouth with four wee teeth. Her chunky arms and legs are jointed at hips and shoulders. She has long blue ribbed socks and molded black slippers with heels. Her only incising is *150.1* on back of her head with *150* on the leg flange. *Her* date is a moot question, too. Probably before 1891.

"Happy Birthday, Tessa."

Sweetie

All Bisque—6 Inch

Sweetie is an excellent quality doll. The bisque is smoother than the other dolls, modeling and tinting more delicate; curved arms and shapely legs more realistic and she has a swivel-neck socket-head. There are two teeth, and her mouth, open in a tiny smile, shows tongue color, too.

Sweetie's lace trimmed cotton dress is a bright blue and is striking with her very long golden hair, mohair, with bangs. She has high white socks and molded high black boots with tiny heels and bright blue tassels. Her sleeping eyes match her dress and tassels. A tiny red garter line borders the top of her socks, and her hat is white lace with a pink bow directly on top.

Sweetie has no marking whatever and could date in the 1880's.

Eleanor-Rose
Turtle Mark Celluloid—5 Inch

ELEANOR-ROSE is all celluloid, and the modeling is good. Her hair is molded in little soft curls about the face and neck. Eyes are painted brown and have a red line above the eye like many of the old chinaheads. Her mouth is closed and ears show; nostril dots, too. She is jointed only at the shoulders; arms are curved. Eleanor's fingers and toes are well defined.

On back of her shoulders is embossed *SCHUTZ-MARKE* with the turtle underneath. Schutz-Marke simply means "Protected Trademark." The dolls with this mark were made by The Rheinische-Gummi-Und-Celluloid Fabric Co. of Mannheim-Neckarau, Germany (Western Zone now, and they are still in business). Eleanor is an oldie—her date, 1889.

This little girl has a dainty white lawn dress with a wide lace collar. Her cap is lace too, with lavender ribbon and bows. Her little boots are made of white silk tied with white silk bows. Undies are very lacy. Everything is handmade and quite old—might be original. All was very yellow with age when she arrived.

See: "Celluloid Dolls" by Jennie L. Abbott in *Dolls 1946*.
"Dolls with the Turtle Trademark" by Luella Hart in the *Antiques Journal*, October, 1955.
"Celluloid Dolls Had Their Day" in *Doll Talk*, July–August, 1961.

GABRIELLE

GABRIELLE

Gabrielle

French Fashion—17½ Inch

THIS lovely lady is a most satisfying doll to own. Her pictures simply do not convey the full extent of her exquisiteness. Would we could all be as daintily beautiful past the age of ninety! She is all original and has an old trunk of clothes and accessories including her own wee calling cards and case. That's how I knew what her name was, my Gabrielle.

These so-called "Fashion Dolls" have varied facial expressions. Some are elegant, just as many look haughty, some smile slightly and a few have a big smile. Then there is Gabrielle's type—with a gentle, sweet, soft expression. Wish I knew the artist who designed her and the maker who produced her—but she is utterly unmarked.

Gabrielle's swivel-necked shoulderhead is pale, smooth bisque. The modeling and tinting is done with delicacy and refinement. Her mouth is closed, large medium-blue blown glass eyes are stationary, inner eye corners and nostrils tinted. Ears are pierced and wires of original blue bead earrings are twisted together inside her head. She has a cork cap and soft brown fine human hair, simply dressed. She came with three sparse long curls hanging in back but she looked shabby so it is now gathered into a net (*Godey's* for 1869) and she is neat and well groomed. Her body is exactly like Yvonne's.

This "Poupée Parisienne" is dressed in medium-blue silk taffeta with tiny black stripes. It is trimmed in very narrow black silk braid. There is a full foundation skirt and beruffled underskirt (both longer in back), a full and complete overskirt with tucked-up bustle pouch and a long-sleeved tight-fitting V-necked jacket, all of the same material. This whole outfit, including undies, everything she could possibly have, is handmade; white cotton lining and wee narrow tapes adjust the fit, like a woman's clothes of the 70's. The *pièce de résistance* is her elegantly designed white horsehair bustle made just like the real ones with those tiny tapes again, for adjustment. Truthfully, it takes almost half an hour to dress this doll. No wonder girls had to have maids in those days!

Gabrielle's Chinese coolie-type white silk hat is trimmed and tied under her chin with narrow black velvet ribbons. It is further secured by a steel cut, decorated hat pin. Her shoes are worth mentioning—black leather boots with tiny heels. They are laced high on her black cotton stockings with the tiniest grommets and metal-tipped shoe laces imaginable.

Let's peek in her old trunk (10 inches wide, 20 inches long and 8½ inches deep). It has a rounded top with hand wrought iron clasp and large iron handle on top. It is covered with horsehide or deerskin bound around the edges with leather and studded with brass tacks. Hinges are heavy leather reinforcements of the outside covering. This trunk is lined with patterned paper, brown and tan with white dots. There is an old fancy oval paper label inside the lid which reads: *Made and sold by Curtis and Coolidge, Main Street, Windsor, Vt.* Since there were two other trunks like this one, only smaller, where I obtained this outfit, it would seem that Curtis and Coolidge exported trunks to France for French dolls. All three trunks and dolls were purchased and brought over here from Paris by the same lady a few years ago.

The most exciting item in Gabrielle's trunk is her lovely lavender brocaded silk taffeta pegnoir. It is cut very full, hangs from the shoulders, floor length, and is almost five inches longer in back. It is trimmed with lace and tiny braid around all edges and there is a three-inch scalloped ruffle of self material around the hemline that is literally festooned with lace and braid. The sleeves are long and bell-shaped with two rows of lace for decoration.

In her picture, you see a silver metal mesh purse and her ivory-handled silk parasol, trimmed with two-inch gold silk fringe.

A glamorous girl, this Gabrielle, my "Barbie" doll of long ago!

Contents of Gabrielle's Old Trunk

1 lavender brocaded taffeta peignoir
1 golden-brown taffeta suit with full black net overskirt and trimming
1 deep-brown brocaded velvet skirt
1 long gold wool coat, very large shawl collar
1 short plaid wool coat (purple, black and green)
1 short black taffeta evening jacket, fringed with black silk, covered with tiny white beads
3 hats with flowers, ribbons and plumes
1 white lace morning cap with long, lacy streamers and seven blue ribbon bows
1 wide, white, fitted lace scarf, crosses in front, hangs several inches
1 pair white kid slippers
1 ivory comb—double edged
1 pink celluloid hairbrush
1 bone handled clothes brush
1 pack of tiny playing cards
1 ivory-covered tiny prayer book with minute metal clasp, printed in French—with pictures, too! ($\frac{7}{8}$ inch by $1\frac{1}{8}$ inches)
1 box of minute envelopes and letter paper, decorated
1 card case with calling cards imprinted "Gabrielle"

2 very old trinket boxes
2 faded photographs (1½″ x 2″) of an old French doll; a toy skin horse
   harnessed. Backs of photos have printed toy store advertisement—
   PERREAU BROS., PARIS (perhaps the one from which Gabrielle
   originally came)

Marie
French (?) All Bisque—7½ Inch

SINCE Marie is unmarked and old,
we can't prove she's French but she looks it. Her beautiful blue blown
glass set eyes, the dainty modeling of nose and closed mouth, the
heavy eyebrows and the unusually fine modeling of her hands all bespeak
a French origin—not to mention the fine quality of her bisque.

Anyway, we do know she's adorable with her little left arm upturned
at the elbow; her chubby stance, one foot ahead of its mate. She has
dimples and fat rolls in all the right places. White ribbed socks with blue
garter line at the top and black two-strap shoes with tiny heels are
molded, then painted. She is jointed at neck, shoulders and hips.

There isn't much left of her blond mohair cap, but it's original and
looks cute peeking out from under her deep-pink silk bonnet. Her undies
are handmade of white cotton with lacy uppers. There is edging on the
panties; tiny buttons and button holes. Her pink silk dress matches the
bonnet. It is ankle length, high-waisted, long-sleeved with wide full
ruffles from the waist in front, across the shoulders and down to the waist
in back. There are two vertical pink satin ribbon bows with streamers in
back and a small ribbon rosette in front. Featherstitching at hemline.
There we are again—very Frenchy. If her clothes are not original, at least
they are very old.

Since envy is too expensive an emotion, guess we'll give it up—but we
can love her, can't we, this *petite Marie?*

Hilda

J. D. Kestner Walker—20 Inch

Please help me, Mommie."

All little girls can strip their dollies. It's the first thing they do with a new doll, if left to their own devices. Putting the clothes back on is another story!

Hilda is a walker. Her mechanism works like Mimi's and she also turns her head from side to side. Her ball-jointed composition body is well modeled; toddler legs dimpled.

Hilda's nice bisque head is quite different. Her face is rather round and so are her large gray-blue sleep-eyes with real lashes. Her chin is dimpled with a fat roll underneath, mouth open, four teeth, nostrils dotted. Some artists capture such a childlike freshness in a doll, and this, Hilda has. Her high coloring gives her an alive, vital look, too.

Her brown human hair wig is parted from ear to ear across the top of her head and pulled back into a one-curl ponytail. Long bangs fall forward in soft ringlets about her face.

Hilda wears a darling old long-sleeved blue and white print apron with a wide sash tied in back. It buttons at the top but is open all the way down the back. There are buttons at the cuffs and a full ruffle on a yoke —both featherstitched in blue; pockets, too. Socks are white cotton ribbed, shoes black patent leather.

There is a Kestner crown label on her throat; *J.D.K.—260* incised on back of her head; *Made in Germany* at the base of her neck. Hilda dates after 1910—when German dolls began to look less stereotyped—perhaps even in the early 20's.

"Coming, Hilda."

Both dolls belong to Mrs. Marianne De Nuñez of Arleta, California.

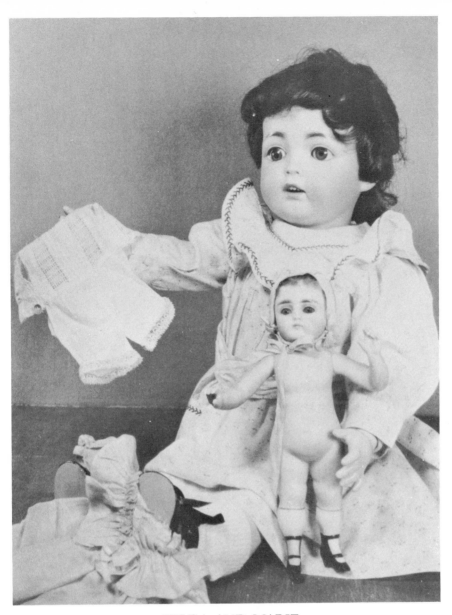

HILDA AND MARIE

"Stowaway"　　JACKIE AND BROWNIE

Jackie
Turtle Mark Celluloid—15 Inch

T<small>HIS</small> chubby toddler has *Made in Germany* on back of his neck, with the turtle mark in the diamond. His hair, eyes and teeth are molded and painted. He has blue eyes, four little white teeth, tiny red gums. He has very nice ears and a cute round baby nose. His entire head is unusually well painted, hair brown, face and neck flesh color with rosy cheeks. You have to feel his head to tell it from wood. No offense, Jackie!

Jackie's pink cloth body is jointed at shoulders and hips. Heavy enclosed cardboard circles fit snugly against matching circles, and head and all are strung with heavy elastic. Quite stout and well proportioned, his body is solidly stuffed with finely shredded paper. The fingers are stitched, thumbs applied separately.

Jackie's little pink wool trousers, silk shirt and green sweater are modern. He wears white shoes and socks and a little white felt polo cap. His date? Probably in the 1920's.

He still doesn't know that Brownie's there!

See: Clara H. Fawcett. *Dolls—A Guide for Collectors*, p. 121.
"Dolls with the Turtle Trademark" by Luella Hart in *Antiques Journal*, October, 1955.

Brownie
Palmer Cox—6 Inch

P<small>ALMER</small> Cox approved this type of Brownie, designed and manufactured by a lady in 1890. It originated from his characters, first created in 1883.

Brownie has a wire frame, head and tight fists of chamois, and a soft cotton body encased in brown silk knit material. The jacket front outline and buttons are painted.

The wire in his legs and arms is slipped between thick woven tape and it can be bent into different angles. He has long pointed pieces of soft leather for feet. His droll little facial features are painted, the eyes heavily enameled. A cunning little lantern hangs on one arm. Bet he doesn't dare light it now!

See: "Palmer Cox, His Brownies and Brownie Dolls" in *American Made Dolls and Figurines*, 1940.
"Palmer Cox and his Brownies" by Ethel Foster in *Antiques Journal*, February, 1955.

Marietta

Pierotti (?) Wax—18 Inch

Marietta's stationary blue eyes are lovely, but some child of long ago has kissed or washed off her lashes and eyebrows! They were set in, a few at a time, as was her soft brown hair. It wasn't moths, since her human hair is still intact under her flowered bonnet of fine straw.

Marietta's dainty dimity dress, with all-over blue pin dots and lavender flowers, is handmade, trimmed with pink braid bows—Kate Greenaway style, with pantalettes, lovely lace and embroidery. It is quaint, but not original. Long lisle stockings are white, slippers, blue satin.

Marietta is all Pierotti, I believe. She is like those waxes pictured and described by Lesley Gordon, right down to the brindle cow hair stuffing. Her head, turned slightly to the right, and shoulderpiece are flesh-colored wax, as are her forearms and lower legs. The shoulders are fastened to the white linen narrow-waisted body by tapes. This tape is threaded through grommet-protected holes in the wax; two in back, two in front. The wax forearms have two protected holes just above the elbow also. Tape passed through these holes has been sewn to the short upper arm which is part of her body. The legs above the knees have a deep groove around the top for attaching to the linen upper leg.

While her wax hands and arms are nice, her legs, feet and tiny toes are more detailed and life-like. The joints are at hips and shoulders, made with machine stitching. Marietta's nose, closed mouth and chin are a bit flat but for a wax doll made well before 1890, she is in very nice condition.

The Pierottis were made in England by the same family from 1790 until 1935. They marked some of their dolls *H. Pierotti* under the hair in back for a while before 1891. Before 1890, the bodies were stuffed with cow hair, later with kapok. Therefore, since Marietta is stuffed with cow hair and unmarked, I deduct her age to be around 80 years, perhaps more. I'm guessing, of course, but that's part of the fun!

See: "The Pierotti Wax Doll" by Lesley Gordon in *Spinning Wheel*, February, 1957. Gwen White. *Dolls of the World*.

MARIETTA

"Time Out"   PITTI-PAT, MIMI, GRETCHEN, HENRIETTA, JUNETTA AND KIPPY

Pitti-Pat
All Bisque—6½ Inch

Pitti-Pat, a trusting soul, stands right behind the pony! To her left is Mimi (described elsewhere) wearing a white party dress.

Pitti-Pat looks as though she might have been designed by Grace G. Drayton. She is googly-eyed (sleeping and side-looking) and cunning. Her fat cheeks are accentuated by the curved lines at each side of her mouth. She has a button nose, a smiling closed mouth and blue eyes quite far apart.

Pitti-Pat dates before 1891 (no markings) and her personal history agrees. Her dress of pink crepe de Chine with full skirt and puffed sleeves is also old.

This little German toddler, jointed at hips and shoulders, has chubby curved arms, separate thumbs and adorable stocky legs. Her knees are dimpled and her white molded short socks are slightly wrinkled. One-strap black slippers with low heels are also molded. Pitti-Pat's short mohair cap is light brown and straight. It's almost a bowl type hair cut but cute on her.

Gretchen
All Bisque—5½ Inch

THIS "Dutchy-looking" youngster, astride the pony, has a Dutch bob, and a stolid, serious expression. Her painted eyes are blue, the nose a bit sharp, mouth closed and a deep dimple in her chin. The bisque is only fair, the tinting faint. Her mohair wig is soft brown. She is wire-jointed at hips and shoulders with curved arms and very pretty cupped hands. Her molded shoes are clover-pink with low heels. Blue line garters top the white ribbed socks.

Gretchen's pink flowered cotton print (such a *tiny* print) is new, lace trimmed and made with a large bib effect front and back, extending out over short sleeves; skirt gathered at the waist. Her white panties have matching narrow lace and extend below the dress a bit.

Incised on Gretchen's back is *Germany 5—296*. Her date then—is sometime after 1891.

Henrietta
Armand Marseille—8½ Inch

HENRIETTA, the tallest doll, came from the same private family as Pitti-Pat. Her fluffy auburn mohair wig is new but otherwise she is all original. Her commercial clothes have never been removed. They are sewn and nailed on, back and front. Near her left ear, in pencil, is the original price mark—*25 cents!*

Henrietta could be dated. At the base of her swivel-neck bisque head is incised *1900—8½*. Above that is the A & M horseshoe mark (but no A & M) and above that, the letters *D E P*. No Germany at that date? No. Well, perhaps it was on the box for she could have had a box, being dressed.

This pretty little girl has fair quality bisque, pale coloring, large dark brown set eyes, an open mouth, three teeth—that's right, three—and a red felt tongue. Her composition body, jointed at hip and shoulder is rather crude, but well proportioned. Black molded slippers have low heels, two straps; white ribbed high socks have pink garter lines.

Her medium blue skirt and large shawl collar are silk, lace trimmed, with a cerise bow and small corsage in front. Her white cotton blouse (blue polka dots) short sleeves, and white panties are lace trimmed, too. All this for a quarter!

Junetta
Colored German Bisque—7 Inch

It was dark-skinned Junetta who remembered to feed the pony. Kippy was water boy.

Junetta's bisque swivel-neck head is colored clear through, not painted as were so many colored dolls. Since her features are not Negroid, perhaps she was meant to represent some other dark skinned race. Incised on back of her head is *Made in Germany, 12/0* and underneath, the initial N. Obviously she was made after 1891 but when? She is a lighter color than many; head and body shade matching perfectly. Her brown glass eyes with darker brown pupils are stationary. She has a sweet expression with open mouth, four teeth, very red lips, eye corners and nostrils tinted. Her black bobbed wig is slightly fuzzy wool of some kind, quite suitable. She wears a cerise hair ribbon. Matching ribbons tie her black shoes.

The fully jointed composition body is like the large German ones, ball joints and all. Thighs, upper and lower arms are wooden; hands and well modeled lower legs and feet are composition. The knees are dimpled, toes and fingers defined.

Because of her color, Junetta was hard to dress but her lace-trimmed dark blue cotton dress with gathered skirt, short sleeves and square neck, becomes her.

See: "Doll Buying in Europe Before World War II" by Luella Hart in *Toy Trader,* March 1954.

Kippy
All Bisque Boy (Japan)—6 Inch

Although made in Japan, Kippy is an American child. His painted golden hair (molded) resembles the hairdo of the Patsy dolls by EFFanBEE of the late twenties and early thirties. Kippy probably dates around that time, too. Incised across his shoulders is *MADE IN JAPAN.*

Kippy has a sweet little face, with closed mouth, real rosy cheeks and painted blue eyes with black pupils. His arms are curved and he has flat-soled one-strap brown slippers, molded and painted. Actually, he could pass for a girl, but his original cotton clothes, factory made, consist of long blue and white striped trousers and a blue and white checked jacket.

Jointed only at the shoulders and hips, Kippy, although independent, would have quite a time mounting a pony with no help!

"Nursery School"   TESSA, ELEANOR, JUNETTA,
GRETCHEN, MAUDIE AND BITSY

"Boys' Toys"   TESSA AND JUNETTA

VANTA BABY

Vanta Baby
Amberg—16 Inch (Seated)

VAN's Nana gave him a sterling silver rattle and curved-handle spoon—suitably engraved, of course. That's the way with grandmas—"Nothing is too good, etc. etc." But you have to admit he's a cutie in his little white piqué rompers and blue and white wool booties.

The Vanta Baby (probably complete with Vanta shirt) was patented on March 22, 1927 (#247,056) by Louis Amberg and Sons, New York, N.Y. This particular specimen is in a fine state of preservation; fat unbleached muslin body as well as composition head, curved arms and very chubby curved legs. He has molded and tinted hair, golden in color, gray-blue metal sleeping eyes with gold-brown real hair lashes and an open-closed mouth with two molded-in upper teeth. He still has rosy cheeks, eye corner and nostril dots and a big smile. His head is on a composition shoulder piece and embossed on the back is: *Vanta Baby—AMBERG.*

Van is stitch-jointed at hips and has a heavy spring running under the shoulderplate joining both arms tightly to the body, although they move easily in a complete circle—when naked, that is!

This big bright fellow who sits up so well by himself on his ample fat rear is from the collection of Mrs. Pat Schoonmaker of North Hollywood, California.

See: "Amberg Dolls" by Elizabeth A. Coleman in *Antique Journal*, April and May, 1962.

SHEPHERDESS AND SHEPHERD

Shepherd and Shepherdess
F. G. French Costume Dolls—12 Inch

As I photographed this pair of little dolls, two things kept running through my mind: Chapter XX from *Wizard of Oz* by L. Frank Baum, called "The Dainty China Country," and the bucolic characters who romp through the rococo 18th century paintings.

I re-read "Oz" Chapter XX (and more!)—checked the paintings and *there* were the dolls, in silks, satins, and velvet; with bodices, breeches and buckles.

These dolls seem identical, yet the bisque socket heads do vary; he has more detail, a dimpled chin, larger set-in blue eyes and deeper color. Not much time was spent sanding either head but they are pretty little French people, as you can see. Their well-proportioned papier-mâché bodies are jointed with wooden pegs at hips and shoulders.

Their clothes are commercially made and original. Both dolls have low-cut black leather shoes, black leather bows and metal buckles. On the soles is C. M. in an oval and #3/0. Both have long red cotton stockings. Her very full overskirt, the band on her white organdy apron and his cap and jerkin are of lovely sky-blue satin. They have white satin blouses, long and full; his long-sleeved, her sleeves bell-shaped. He has a collar tied with a red cord and tassel, like his hat; there is lace at her neckline. Her red satin skirt and bodice are trimmed with black velvet bands; bodice laced with narrow blue silk ribbon. His velvet pants are that beautiful ruby shade often seen in French doll clothes. Their fuzzy hair is some sort of ivory-colored wool.

Both dolls are incised *F.G.* in an oval on back of their necks. The girl is marked *F. 4 G.*; the boy, *F. G.* with #4 below. Probably made by Gautier (Gaultier) in 1885–1900.

These dancers belong to Mrs. Dolores Devine of Culver City, California.

See: Elizabeth A. Coleman. *Dolls—Makers and Marks*, pp. 22 and 23.
    Luella Hart. *Complete French Doll Directory*, p. 56.

Marie Thérèse

P. D. French Bisque—26 Inch

MARIE Thérèse looks taller than she really is. Perhaps it's her handsome high-peaked French bonnet with brown velvet bows on top and lacy frou-frou under the brim. Wish you could see the beautiful maroon satin of Marie's little coat and bonnet brim. Her dress is changeable gold taffeta with brown stripes. The low-waisted skirt is shirred very full. There is pleated lace at the neck and at the bottom of her striped cuffs and a large striped bow on her coat, in back, over her hips.

Marie Thérèse's smooth bisque head is very pale, her tinting delicate and dark brown blown-glass eyes simply enormous. There are eye and nostril dots, gold ear drops, fat cheeks and a closed mouth. Her golden brown wavy human hair (cork pate) lies softly on her shoulders and there are heavy bangs.

Marie's well-shaped hand, just disappearing into her brown fur muff, is metal; looks like pewter. Long slender fingers, each one modeled separately, are still perfect. The fine French body, fully articulated, has a defunct voice box in a papier-mâché torso. Ball-jointed arms and upper legs are wooden; lower legs papier-mâché. Marie's socks are maroon; brown kid slippers have rosettes on the toes and E. J. stamped in the sole. Incised on the back of her head is P. 5 D. She looks like an oldie. Could she have been made by Petit and Dumontier around 1880?

All of Marie's undies have lace flounces three inches long and beading with narrow pink ribbon running through—too pretty to be hidden! Actually, every now and then something *does* show, but who cares?

All three lovelies are from the collection of Mrs. Ellery C. Thorpe of Glendale, California. Rosalie, center is described elsewhere.

See: Elizabeth A. Coleman. *Dolls—Makers and Marks*, p. 57.
Luella Hart. *Complete French Doll Directory*, p. 30.

Suzette

Bru Jeune—23 Inch

THE blond curly-headed lamb under the pale turquoise corded silk bonnet, complete with curtain or apron, is Suzette. Her Bru loveliness is so apparent, she really wouldn't

MARIE THÉRÈSE, ROSALIE AND SUZETTE

need to be marked *Bru Jne 9* on swivel head or bisque shoulderplate, but she is. Her body is exactly like Fanchon's with one exception—her pretty arms are wooden and hand carved.

Suzette's bisque head is smooth, beautifully modeled and delicately tinted. Mouth closed, inner eye corners and nostrils tinted, ears pierced. Her full-orbed eyes, blown glass and stationary, are medium-blue with large pupils.

Her lovely new silk dress with its panel of full shirring down the front, low waist and pleated skirt, is pale turquoise. There are lots of wide lace flounces and trims, to say nothing of the fullness at the back! The bonnet has more than its share of lacy ruffles, too.

Suzette's new wig is wheaten in color and very fine textured. It hangs in long curls all around her shoulders. The short bangs are wavy.

SALLY

Sally
Unmarked French Bisque—15 Inch

Sally is a love with her delicate features and soft brown sleeping eyes. Her swivel-neck head and shoulder-plate are pale bisque of fine quality. Fat cheeks and dimpled double chin give her an appealing expression. Her mouth is closed, ears applied.

Sally is all original—blond mohair wig (cork pate) included. She wears bangs with a few little curls around her neck. Her body is white kid with three vertical seams on the lower back; gussets at rump, knees and elbows. Her arms are bisque below the elbow. Hands turn back at the wrist; cupped fingers and hands are well defined even to the fat rolls in her palms. Sally's feet are kid, the toes are stitched and she wears white ribbed cotton stockings and black shoes with brown uppers in front.

Her old-fashioned light blue wool dress, pleated at the waist, is almost floor length, with bell sleeves and boat neck. It is trimmed with bands of black velvet—two rows on the full skirt, and one on the sleeves and neck. Dainty white tucked undersleeves come to her wrists.

Sally's darling white cap is the long-aproned sunbonnet type, of cross-barred dimity—lace edged. There is a tiny self-bow at the back of the neck.

As Sally is unmarked, her age cannot be proven, but wouldn't you say she is about 80 years old? That's almost too old to use a spinning wheel—yet she looks too young to know how! A puzzlement! Well—if she could and would, it would probably work well. The treadle really moves; the wheel goes whirring; its age about the same as hers.

Sally and the wheel belong to Mrs. Ruby Sligh of Glendale, California.

GENELLE AND BEULAH

Genelle
All Bisque (Reproduction)—7¼ Inch

"G ENELLE, the water's getting cold, come on!" Genelle couldn't care less. She intends to put her baby in the boat first.

This child is a lovely reproduction of a 1920 Heubach-type toddler by Marianne De Nuñez of Arleta, California. Incised on her smooth bisque shoulders is *Marianne—1962.*

Genelle is delicately tinted and well modeled. Her mouth is closed; brown eyes look to the side. Her molded blond bobbed hair, black one strap slippers and short white ribbed socks are cunning. She is pink tinted at knees, elbows, breasts and backs of hands. The third and fourth fingers of each hand are joined, the rest of her fingers outspread. She is jointed at shoulders and hips.

The old china accessories belong to Thelma-Marie. The ceramic tub came from a thrift shop, just in time.

Beulah
All Bisque—8½ Inch

B EULAH is very old, German, but unmarked except for *208-7* way up under her wig and the same on the inside flange of legs and arms. Her bisque is fair but does not compare in color or quality with the reproduction doll "Genelle."

She is pretty, though, with brown sleeping eyes, open mouth, four tiny teeth, chin dimple, dots in eye corners and nostrils. Her new auburn mohair goes nicely with her eyes, eyebrows and unusually long painted eyelashes.

Jointed at hips and shoulders, she has molded black one-strap slippers with heels and long white ribbed socks with blue garter line. Her fingers are well defined, slightly cupped with the thumbs separate.

Beulah now belongs to Miss Arax Arklin of Granada Hills, California.

Jacques & Jean Paul
S.F.B.J. Toddler Twins—15 Inch

A wise mother is raising these French character babies. They are fraternal twins but she treats each one as an individual in his own right—advised by modern child psychologists. See their darling outfits, similar and equally adorable, yet different. Jacques, on the left has a tan leather tam; Jean Paul's is dark red velvet. Jacques' "Buster Brown" suit with large sailor collar edged in real Irish crochet is white cotton gabardine. Jean Paul's suit of fine wool flannel is beige with tiny red stripes and has a diagonal closing, piped in dark red silk. Cuffs and large circular collar are red velvet. Jacques has white cotton socks and black patent leather tie shoes. Jean wears red lace socks and dear little red sandals. Both boys' bloomers, bloused at the knee, show below their tunics.

The twins' bodies are alike: short-coupled, fully ball-jointed toddler-type; of composition. Upper and lower arms are of wood. Jacques has a round red, white and blue sticker on his back which reads, in part, (the rest is torn) *Fabrication—Paris*—with *S.F.B.J.* in the center. I guess Jean Paul's soaked off in the bath!

Both boys have nice quality bisque heads well modeled and nicely tinted. Both have dimples, smiles, set blue eyes, nostril dots and two molded teeth.

Jacques' eyes are fuller and darker blue than his brother's. He also has the open-closed mouth and the biggest grin, corner eye dots, dimple in chin. Jean's dimples are in his cheeks; little bisque tongue on a spring, mouth open. Jean talks more. Check the picture, he even uses his hands to sell Jacques an idea. Jacques' mop of golden ringlets is a nice foil for his brother's straight red-brown boyish bob. Human hair on both.

Incised on back of Jean's head is:

23
S.F.B.J.
251
PARIS
6

Jacques' head has:

23
S.F.B.J.
236
PARIS
6

JACQUES AND JEAN PAUL

Both boys date in the 1900's, perhaps before 1915. S.F.B.J. is an abbreviation of the firm name *Société Française de Fabrication de Bébés et Jouets*. Freely translated it is *French Corporation for the Manufacture of Dolls and Toys*. This corporation was formed in 1899.

The wise mother of these tykes is Mrs. Ellery C. Thorpe of Glendale, California.

See: "Jumeau and the Golden Age of Dolls" in *Doll Talk*, November–December, 1959. Luella Hart. *Complete French Doll Directory*, p. 60.

JILL AND FLAPPER

Jill

Simon & Halbig—13 Inch

Tʜɪꜱ is Jill, child of the Twenties. She looks about ten years old, and is she well dressed! Everything she has, except tam, is original and handmade including leather moccasin-type loafers. Red knee-length socks and mittens and tan sweater are hand knit of fine wool on the tiniest of needles. Dainty white panties and slip have matching embroidered edges, and the pleated plaid skirt is fine gingham. Jill's princess style soft gray-blue flannel coat with covered buttons is a dream—exquisitely tailored, inside and out.

Her socket-head is high quality bisque, perfectly modeled and tinted, with dainty nose, nostrils dotted, tiny open mouth with four teeth, and large sleeping eyes the color of her coat. Jill's mohair is medium brown, a Dutch bob, topped by a red hand crocheted tam.

Jill has a composition body, slender and well proportioned, jointed at neck, shoulders, hips and *above* the knees. This is the knee joint used so much after World War I. The entire doll and her clothes are in beautiful condition.

Jill's "Flapper" doll is a bisque shoulderhead doll-house doll with arms and lower legs of bisque. Black slippers with heels are modeled and painted. Her bisque, modeling and tinting are good for a small doll—just five inches high. She looks to be in her late teens. Her cloth body is stuffed with sawdust. She has stitch-jointed hips and elastic-jointed arms. Flapper's long-waisted dress is pale green silk with gold lace set in above the hemline. She has brown bobbed mohair and a strand of gold beads. All are original and typically done for her era.

Jill is incised on back of her head, *Simon Halbig, S & H* and the number 5. Flapper is marked *701* and *14/0*. Both were made in Germany. They must have had paper labels at one time.

Dolls and all accessories are from the collection of Marianne De Nuñez of Arleta, California.

Michèle
Eden-Bébé Walker—23 Inch

H<small>EY</small>, there, you black-eyed Parisienne, what's your hurry?—A picnic?—Just you and the lamb?—Well, have fun."

Michèle's little tan cotton print of multicolor flowers is old and all handmade. It hangs from a lined yoke and has a full ruffle around the bottom as well as around the high neck. It is just the frock for picnics—washable and all that! Her socks are white cotton; shoes are black patent with buckle and ribbon ties.

Michèle's head is the palest bisque I ever saw. Any paler and it would be white. There is tinting, but ever so delicate except for the large color dots (inner eye corners and nostrils) and the area above the eyes. Here, the tinting is quite pronounced or at least seems so by contrast with the whiteness of her skin. Also, she has the longest, thickest, blackest painted lashes! All this combines to give her enormous black eyes a luminous quality, and an intense expression. A beautiful French child! Her mouth is open with six teeth—handy for picnics!

Dark brown human hair, slightly curled, hangs longer in back than in front where it curls softly about her face and neck. The ears are tinted and pierced, but she has no earrings. Do you suppose she lost them running to picnics?

Michèle walks—like Mimi—and also turns her head from side to side. The mechanism is attached to a wooden block in her neck, though, instead of running up to a crossbar in the head. The end result, however, is the same.

Michèle's upper and lower arms are turned wooden shafts secured by heavy elastic cord. Body, hands and straight legs (no knee joints) are hard, dark material so much used by the French. The entire doll was made by Fleischmann and Bloedel. The walking mechanism is a variation of patent #234005—issued November 20, 1894. This dates Michèle in the 1890's. The back of her head is incised *EDEN BÉBÉ—Paris—9*.

The little lamb who has green glass eyes in his composition face can lower his head and say, "Baa-baa." He is on a red wooden platform with metal wheels; in perfect condition and unmarked. He is undoubtedly a German toy—made sometime before the turn of the century. His original price of $1.00 is penciled underneath the wooden platform.

MICHÈLE

Wouldn't we like to buy him for that?

"*Au revoir, petits agneaux!*"

Michèle and lamb are from the collection of Mrs. Marianne De Nuñez of Arleta, California.

See: Elizabeth A. Coleman, *Dolls—Makers and Marks*, p. 21.
  Luella Hart. *Complete French Doll Directory*, p. 109.

CHARLOTTE AND PATRICIA

Patricia

Parian Bisque—12½ Inch

PATRICIA is an early parian shoulder-head, so pale she is almost white; delicately modeled and lightly tinted. With her closed mouth, eye and nostril dots, blue paperweight eyes and molded golden curls, curls, curls, she looks like the small girls in the old children's books. Frankly, I could easily covet this one!

Pat's hands and lower arms are bisque, tinted and dimpled. The rest of the body is white kid, with gussets at hips, knees and elbows. She is chubby all over and inclined to be slightly pigeon-toed. On her it's cute! She has brown lacy stockings and black tie slippers on those afore mentioned toes.

Patricia's large bertha and elbow flounces are ivory silk lace. Her high-waisted dress is ivory silk, very sheer, with a self-pattern of openwork stripes. The belt is lace insertion which also decorates the top of the hemline. Blue French knots edge the insertion. There are narrow pale blue ribbon bows at the neck and on each elbow.

Patricia's 3½ inch "Frozen Charlotte" dolly takes my eye, too. She's a honey and not a day younger than 110 years, a decade or so earlier than Patricia, her mommie. Dolly's personal history bears this out.

Charlotte's black hairdo is like hundreds of the Greiners and Pre-Greiners, parted in the center with sausage curls around the back. Her clever off-shoulder dress is apricot silk with black velvet bands and sash.

Dolly is unmarked but Patricia has 890 #5 on back of her shoulder-plate. Both of these "delectable collectables" were made in Germany, and found their way into the collection of Mrs. Milo Hill of Pacoima, California.

CEDRIC

Cedric
Blond Bisque—15 Inch

CEDRIC certainly takes his ease in the new Chinese chair. All the kiddies love that chair—they squabble over it, frequently! Flirt, the parrot, gives them an argument—he thinks it's *his* chair.

Cedric is dressed in a brown velvet suit with knee length trousers and Eton jacket. There are brown silk tassels at the knees. His white blouse has lovely lace at cuffs and on his collar, and he sports a lace jabot with three buttons down the center. His high laced shoes look like elk-skin.

Cedric's bisque shoulderhead turns slightly to the right. He is exquisitely modeled with blond molded hair and large stationary dark brown glass eyes. The bisque is smooth and delicately tinted, mouth closed, nostrils and eye corners colored. His body is of unbleached cotton, sawdust stuffed, jointed at shoulders, hips and knees. Cedric's hands and lower arms are bisque, fingers somewhat cupped, not too well defined. *Germany 30/B2* is incised on his shoulderplate in back. His date perhaps in the early 1890's. Who knows more definitely?

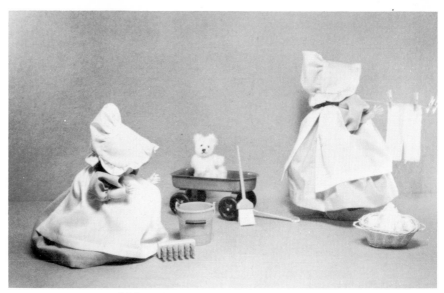

"Chores"   MOLLIE AND MAY

"Tea Party"   MOLLIE, KATE AND MAY

Sunbonnet Babies

Madame Alexander "Wendy"—8 Inch

Molly and May have invited Katie over to have a tea party—if May can find the spoons and napkins. Katie brought her tiny white Steiff teddy bear, and he's included, too.

These little modern hard plastic dolls, the cutest ever, are all "Wendy" from the Alexander-kins, Inc., line. They were first produced in 1953, and are still available. Their Saran wigs are appropriately styled and come in all shades. They are jointed at hips, knees, shoulders and neck and walk while turning head from side to side, using the same principle as "Mimi." The modeling on these delicately tinted Madame Alexander dolls, with their closed mouths and sleeping eyes, is exquisite. In my opinion, the matte finish, hard plastic dolls of this line are among the loveliest on the market today.

Molly, May and Katie are dressed in lovely pastel colors with white aprons, all copied by a friend from the Sunbonnet Babies Primer of 1902, written by Eulalie Osgood Grover. How wise of the artist, Bertha Corbett Melcher, not to show their faces. Makes them far more intriguing, don't you think?

You can get a good look at Wendy and Billie, her twin, in the picture "Christmas Morning."

See: "Sunbonnet Babies and Overall Boys" by Georgia S. Chamberlain in *Spinning Wheel*, April, 1955.
"Sunbonnet Babies Mug" by Georgia S. Chamberlain in *Hobbies*, July, 1954.

"Christmas Morning"   WENDY AND BILLY

ANNE SHIRLEY AND WENDY-ANN

"Fetch"   WENDY-ANN

Wendy-Ann

Madame Alexander—13½ Inch

Mop's passion for ball playing runs the legs off Wendy-Ann. No wonder she is so slender and supple! She bends and turns at the waist as well as being jointed at hips, shoulders and neck. She is all original from blond human hair to black slippers. Her light blue cotton dress with white embroidered trim bears the Alexander label. She has white socks and lacy white underclothes. Her slender composition body is embossed on the back: *WENDY-ANN— MME. ALEXANDER—NEW YORK.*

Wendy's head is also composition, delicately tinted, with shading above her green closing eyes which have real lashes. Her nails, elbows and knees are tinted. She has a tiny closed mouth, a slightly pointed chin and her long bob curls gracefully around face and neck. She is a pretty, dainty, realistic looking little girl of about ten years.

Wendy-Ann was first produced in 1938—this date obtained directly from the Alexander Co. They also made a composition head with molded hair and painted blue eyes. While the bodies and size are the same and the hairdo similar—somehow this last girl looks older—perhaps in the early teens.

Wendy dances with Anne Shirley who wears her original "Later Carolina Settlement" dress (1685). In this outfit, Anne Shirley is a replica of one of the series of Effanbee dolls depicting the "Romance of American Fashions"—1492 to 1939. These historically accurate costume dolls, 30 in all, were an exhibition series produced in 1939 at a cost of $30,000. They were displayed in leading stores around the country.

Anne Shirley (15 inch) has the same type body as the 21-inch doll, described before. She has light brown human hair, center-parted with a roll on each side of her face and long curls over each shoulder. Her painted eyes are brown, mouth closed; eye corner and nostril dots.

Anne Shirley's dress is yellow cotton broadcloth with three rows of lace around the bottom; sleeves ruffled and puffed. The overskirt and bodice are a red, yellow and blue-flowered cotton print, trimmed with blue bows. Pantalettes are ruffled soft muslin. Long white silk stockings and white slippers complete the costume.

On her wrist is a metal heart-shaped tag with *Effanbee Durable Dolls* on both sides, first used in 1924 or 1925. All statistics on *both* Anne Shirley's are directly from the Effanbee Doll Co.

Wendy and Anne belong to Mrs. Pat Schoonmaker of North Hollywood, California.

See: Clara H. Fawcett. *Dolls, A Guide for Collectors*, pp. 75 and 78.

Hey Boy

J. D. Kestner Chinese Baby—13½ Inch (seated)

This precocious little guy who trains horses so early in life, appears here to ask questions and find answers. *Germany—243—J.D.K.* is incised under his wig. *Made in Germany* in red ink appears just below the neckline on his body.

Hey Boy's head is first quality bisque with good Chinese features and the painting is right. The entire doll is tinted a soft buff shade and his rosy cheeks are very appealing. His brown slanting eyes (sleeping) have color dots in inner corners; nostrils dotted, too. The black bobbed human hair is typical of many oriental children. His sweet little smiling mouth has a red bisque tongue on a spring, plus two upper teeth. His curved-leg composition body, jointed at shoulders and hips, has well-defined fingers and toes—big toes upturned.

Hey Boy's gold silk jacket, trimmed in dark blue braid, has gold silk frogs down the front. Trousers are plum colored satin—silk shoes are blue and gold, probably copies of his original clothes.

Most of these oriental character dolls—curved-leg, toddler and older (also put out by A&M, S&H, K&R, Heubach, etc.) are believed to have been first brought out in the early 1900's and produced at least until World War I put a cap on Germany's doll supremacy.

The few references to this doll in doll books and periodicals class it as "Oriental"—almost without exception. This is fine as far as it goes, but wouldn't it be fun to know the truth? Perhaps the manufacturers *didn't* distinguish between Chinese, Japanese, Korean, etc. If this can be proven—well and good. But do we have to go on straddling fences or can we flush out some *documented* information?

Who has an original box? What is printed on it? Have you a pamphlet, a brochure, or an old catalog giving the facts? When *was* this doll first produced? Opinions are interesting, and from enough of them we get a consensus. However, a consensus is not necessarily the truth. Remember how long everyone was sure the world was flat!

I photographed the same Kestner baby (slightly smaller size) in the Alice Schott collection, Santa Barbara Museum of Art, and a card in the case reads: "Chinese Baby—Photographed in Chinatown, San Francisco and sent to Germany and made by Kestner before the first World War. The clothing was copied from that belonging to a baby born in Chinatown in Santa Barbara before the first World War." Checking with the curator and Mrs. Schott elucidated nothing further.

"Teaching Tricks"   HEY BOY AND YUM

This information ties in nicely, however, with the remark made by a Chinese woman to her husband and children who were admiring the same Kestner baby (*still* smaller size) in Shirley Temple's collection in the Los Angeles County Museum: "My mother knew the family of the Chinese baby who was the model for this doll. She told me all about it." Wish I could have talked to the mother!

"Audition"   FLEURETTE

Fleurette
Bru Jeune—Nursing—14½ Inch

THIS theatrical-looking young harpist tried out for one of the "I-Know-a-Secret" shows and made it. Congratulations are in order!

Fleurette's entire body is exactly like Fanchon's—including paper label. Her head in back is incised *Bru Jne*; left back shoulder also incised *Bru Jne* and N.4 T on the right. Her lovely bisque is pale, lightly tinted, even eye and nostril dots. Her big brown blown-glass set eyes and her round open mouth give her a slightly surprised look. Her cork headpiece supports a new dark golden human hair wig and an enormous hat, decorated with red silk ribbon and matching ostrich plume. Pierced ears have diamond (come now!) earrings.

Her jacket, pleated and much longer in back, has a long loose panel at either side, trimmed with a red bow. Both hat and jacket are of heavy ribbed silk material, bright red. This jacket has very wide lapels and is double breasted, fastened with four brass flower buttons. The upper sleeves are large puffs, lower sleeves are of the skirt material with full lace cuffs.

The skirt, pleated from the side fronts all around the back, is a heavy silk print. The ivory ground has colorful prints of children, wearing 1880-style clothing. They are seated in balloon baskets borne aloft by brightly colored butterflies. Only the French could think up something like this!

The entire suit is lined and there is an attached, pleated underskirt, lace trimmed. Underneath, she wears an original chemise trimmed with red stitching and embroidery. All her clothes are old and commercially made except her white crocheted stockings. Her old French white kid slippers have buckles and bows.

Now I ask you, could this very theatrical-looking young lady be a nursing baby doll?

Yes, she is, or rather, used to be. I quote with permission from the June, 1963, list of Antique Dolls from Virginia R. Lake, Paris, France:

"34—Jointed NURSING BRU, 20". Her head is marked *Bru Jne 8*, and the body marked *Bébé Bru No8*. She has big blue feathered eyes, round open mouth, new brown wig and a squeak body with pull strings. She wears her beautiful original long white baby dress over long white slip, lavishly trimmed with tiny pleats, ruffles, insertions of lace and embroidery, with bonnet to match. She has her original glass nursing bottle with 'ivory' nipple, marked *Bébé Téteur, Bru Jeune*, a very rare accessory and proof that the doll is meant to nurse and not to whistle!

This charming doll's big eyes and open mouth, give her a natural expression of wonder and astonishment. The rubber suction cup inside the head has become hardened with age."

This 20-inch Bru is now in a private collection in Missouri.

Fleurette has a wing-type key on the back of her neck, fastened to the bent rod which used to depress the rubber bladder or bulb inside her head. This rod curves over the bladder and is anchored in the nose cavity with plaster of paris. It still turns a bit, but long ago, when the key was turned clockwise, the rod would have almost completely collapsed the bladder. Turning the key counter clockwise thereby allowing the bladder to return to its original shape, would have created a vacuum inside the bladder. This vacuum would have drawn any liquid in through the tiny hole in the doll's mouth. The bladder could be emptied by again turning the key clockwise, collapsing the bladder and expelling its contents.

Credit Marianne De Nuñez of Arleta, California, for the enlightening information in the *following* paragraph.

The circle and dot found on many marked and unmarked Brus, both open and closed mouth, come from the mold. It is a locating mark to indicate where the hole was to be cut for the rod to go through for the nursing Bru. If the mold was old and much used, the circle would be faint and often only part of it, a crescent was visible. The circle can still be seen (or the crescent part of it) on many nursing Brus since the hole was made *within* the circle.

Fleurette has a faint crescent remaining—the dot is gone, of course. Yvette (described elsewhere) has a full circle and dot mold mark but was not equipped to be a nursing baby, after all. She must have lived on love!

See: "French Doll Patents" by Luella Hart in *Antique Journal*, October, 1960.
    Elizabeth A. Coleman. *Dolls—Makers and Marks*, pp. 8–10.

FLEURETTE

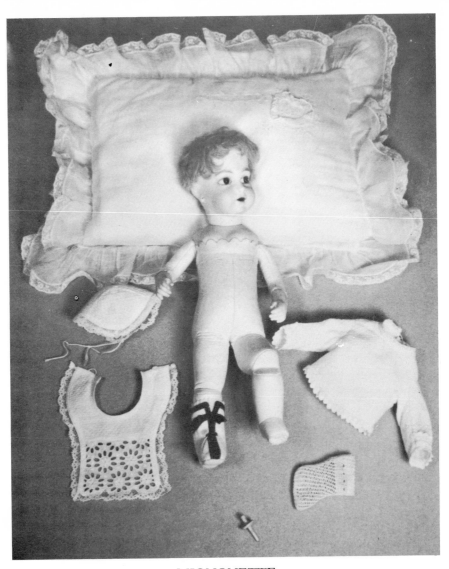

MIGNONETTE

Mignonette
Bru Jeune—Nursing—13 Inch

IMAGINE my joy when a dear little nursing Bru appeared on the scene several months after writing the preceding vignette on Fleurette! This new baby is incised *Bru Jne—2* on back of her head, *Bru Jne* on her left shoulder blade and *No 2* on the right.

Adorable Mignonette has her original hair—a golden baby cap of goat skin—original ivory or bone nursing nipple, original clothing and arrived in her original box!

Mignonette's lovely little face closely resembles Fleurette's—the same full-blown brown threaded eyes, open mouth, smooth bisque, dainty features and delicate tinting. She has pierced ears and a cork pate. Her body is of fine white kid, made exactly like that of Yvette, and in mint condition.

Mignonette is dressed in the manner of most all French new-borns (even today), with long sleeved vest, wrap-around, bib, bonnet and high bootees. All her clothes are made of soft white cotton piqué, fleece-lined, trimmed with lace and embroidery.

The bonnet is a small fitted cap, edged with narrow lace. It ties with tiny tapes. The wrap-around is simply a straight piece of material 9¼ inches wide by 12⅜ inches long, embroidered at the bottom. It wraps around under the arms and buttons with three tiny three-hole buttons in the back. The vest and fitted bib also fasten in back with wee three-hole buttons. The bootees are piped around the top and down the front with narrow dark red tape and laced with matching red ribbon. These are worn over French lace socks. The whole outfit has a very tailored look—unusual on a baby doll. Dressed, Mignonette reminds me of the old candy box baptismal dolls given as souvenirs at christening parties!

It must be mentioned that Mignonette came with the familiar old split drawers (original, too) of fine white material, lace edged. They fasten in back with a tiny tape drawstring. This is not a practical garment for new-borns, so perhaps it was a bid for modesty! The original dressmaker probably thought diapers would be too bulky on so small a doll.

There are three labels on her green cardboard box. On top of the lid is the store label. It translates:

THE BLUE DWARF
27, Boulevard des Capucines
TOYS AND GAMES
Specializing in Dolls and Dressed Bébés (child dolls)
E. CHAVIERE
27, Boulevard des Capucines (across from the Grand Hotel)
PARIS

On the inside of the box lid are two drawings, complete with directional arrows, showing the nursing mechanism and how it works. Underneath are complete instructions in *seven* languages. The photographed enlargement of the upper half shows the French, Spanish and English versions. The remaining are Italian, German, Portuguese and Russian. Both labels are white, printed in black ink.

The box-end label is buff color, printed in gold and translates:

Exhibited for the first time in 1878
SILVER MEDAL
SUCKING BABY
PATENTED—Without Guarantee of Government

Box Top Label

Top Half of Inside Label

Mignonette's nursing nipple can be seen in her undressed photograph just below her feet. The longer, narrower part used to fit through her lips into a narrow hole in the bladder (now shrunken). The knob end has a few remaining specks of the rubber tube which used to fit over it and then extend down through the cork in the bottle neck and onto a glass tube. Wish I had the bottle, too!

Needless to say, Fanchon is entranced with her new baby sister!

Box End Label

Label Inside Box Lid

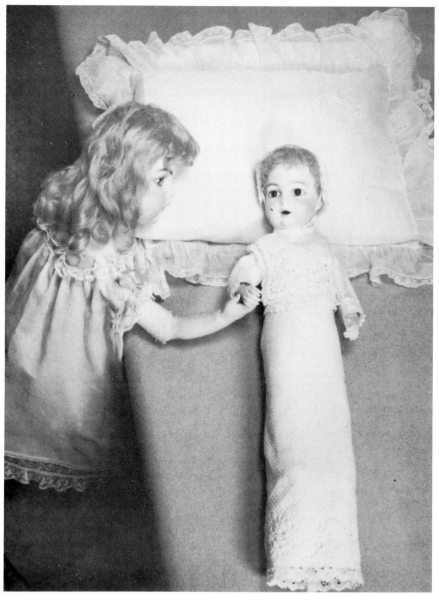

"Enchantment"   FANCHON AND MIGNONETTE

Illustration from Children's Book, Circa 1887

SELECTED BIBLIOGRAPHY

BOOKS

von Boehn, Max. *Dolls and Puppets*. Revised Edition. Boston: Charles T. Branford Co., 1956.

Coleman, Elizabeth A. *Dolls—Makers and Marks*. Washington: Coleman, 1963.

Coleman, Evelyn, Elizabeth and Dorothy. *The Age of Dolls*. Washington: Coleman, 1965.

Davies, Nina S. *The Jumeau Doll Story*. New Orleans: Davies, 1957.

Doll Collectors of America, Inc. Boston:
American Made Dolls and Figurines—1940.
American Made Dolls and Figurines (Supplement)—1942.
Dolls—1946.
Doll Collectors Manual—1949.
Doll Collectors Manual—1956–1957.
Doll Collectors Manual—1964.

Fawcett, Clara H. *Dolls, A New Guide for Collectors*. Boston: Charles T. Branford Co., 1964.

Fawcett, Clara H. *On Making, Mending and Dressing Dolls*. Washington: Hobby House Press, Reissued 1963.

Fisher, Elizabeth A. *Doll Stuff, Again*. Middletown, Conn.: Fisher, 1961.

Freeman, Ruth S. *Encyclopedia American Dolls*. Watkins Glen, N.Y.: Century House, 1962.

Gerken, Jo Elizabeth. *Wonderful Dolls of Wax*. Lincoln, Nebr.: Doll Research Associates, 1964.

Hart, Luella. *Directory of British Dolls*. Oakland: Hart, 1964.

Hart, Luella. *Directory of German Dolls*. Oakland: Hart, 1964.

Hart, Luella. *Complete Directory of French Dolls*. Oakland: Hart, 1965.

Holton, Gladys Reid. *A Monograph on Metal Doll Heads*. Penfield, N.Y.: Genesee Valley Doll Collectors Club.

Horine, Maude M. *Memories of Rose O'Neill*. Revised Edn., 1954.

McClintock, Inez and Marshall. *Toys in America*. Washington: Public Affairs Press, 1961.

Ruggles, Rowena Godding. *The One Rose*. Oakland: Ruggles, 1964.

MAGAZINES

Antiques Journal. Uniontown, Pa.
Doll News. United Federation of Doll Clubs, Inc., Rochester, N.Y.
Doll Talk. Kimport Dolls, Independence, Mo.
Hobbies. Lightner Publishing Corp., Chicago, Ill.
Spinning Wheel. Hanover, Pa.
Toy Trader. Elizabeth A. Fisher, Middletown, Conn.

Index